POLICE CORRUPTION

Donald Campbell

Barry Rose Law Publishers Limited
Little London
Chichester

POLICE CORRUPTION

ISBN 1 902681 29 0

Barry Rose Law Publishers Limited
Little London
Chichester
West Sussex

Contents

Note to the Code of Conduct
Police (Conduct) Regulations April 1999

The principal duties of those who hold the office of constable are the protection of life and property, the preservation of the Queen's peace, and the detection of criminal offences. To fulfil these duties they are granted extraordinary powers; the public and the police service therefore have the right to expect the highest standards of conduct from them.

Jack Straw

Author's Profile

Donald Campbell, born in Belfast in 1928, joined the Metropolitan Police in 1948 after a short period of National Service as an engineer in the submarine service.

Transferring to the Hertfordshire Constabulary, he retired after some 27 years in the rank of Detective-Inspector having been engaged in fraud and corruption investigation for some years.

Called to the Bar in 1976, he practised in the criminal courts in London and the Home Counties until retiring in the year 2000. He was appointed as a Chairman of the Financial Services Act Tribunal and served in that part-time office until retirement.

Previous publications include:

The Investigation of Fraud, 1st and 2nd edition (Barry Rose)
Police: The Exercise of Power (Macdonald & Evans)
International Maritime Fraud (Ellen & Campbell) (Sweet & Maxwell)

Acknowledgements

Many people have helped in the preparation of this book, sometimes unwittingly, and I owe them all a debt of gratitude. In particular Sir Robert Mark and Mr Peter Ryan who have allowed me to use material from their published work. *The Daily Telegraph, The Times* and the *Sydney Morning Herald* have allowed me to use short passages from their newspapers, as has the Press Officer of the Metropolitan Police, New Scotland Yard.

I am particularly grateful to Stuart and Robert Campbell who, by reading the manuscript and offering their professional advice, have saved me from many mistakes, to David and Paul Campbell for their contributions and to other members of my family who have tolerated my frequent progress reports with patience.

Introduction

Most people know the old cliché about power corrupting but the quotation from which it stems is usually misquoted. The original words of William Pitt in 1770 were that ... "Unlimited power is apt to corrupt the minds of those who possess it," whilst Baron Acton, in the 19th century and in typical lawyer-like fashion, expanded the notion into ... "Power tends to corrupt and absolute power corrupts absolutely." But enough of clichés and hoary old philosophy and to the subject in hand.

This book is about corruption among police officers of almost every rank and may possibly cause some resentment among those of them who see no need for a public spotlight to be focused upon it. To them I would say that corruption is a crime tending to lurk in the darkest of recesses where it breeds like some virulent disease, ultimately proving fatal to public trust in the police service. All those officers, the vast majority, who carry out their work honestly can take comfort from the fact that a similar book on political life would need to be at least three times as long. And they would surely see the need to light up that particular area.

Whilst the book is about "bent" policemen and those who use them for their own ends, it inevitably contains some reference to relevant law and various technical bits; however, these have been relegated to appendices at the end where readers who need a starting point for more detailed study may browse.

It is intended for the general reader as well as professionals because the study is one of human beings and their failings; of dyed in the wool villains, porn merchants and drugs dealers; of attempts to kill police officers who came too close to corrupt colleagues evil activities; and of the self-protecting screens erected around highly placed offenders both inside and outside the police.

In the main, the book concentrates on three services ... the Metropolitan Police as the largest, with its responsibility for a huge and culturally diverse London population, and the New South Wales Police, stigmatised by the press as the most corrupt police service in Australia. That label has now, in the year 2000, largely been shaken off by a vigorous and continuing programme of reform. Finally, it examines the cyclical problems of the New York City Police; largest of the three with its deeply entrenched history of corrupt practices.

The most that any book on corruption can do is to present a snapshot of the situation at a particular time because, almost daily, instances of corruption or initiatives to control it are brought into the public arena. However, a look back to the early years of all three services, the recurring scandals over more than a century, and the Herculean efforts at control by some of those in authority may help to provide a lead into the future.

Donald Campbell
Gray's Inn, London

Statutes

United Kingdom

Australia

Decided cases

Cooper v. Slade (1857) 6 H.L. Cas. 746; *R. v. Wellburn* 69 Cr. App. R. 254 CA. Defines corruption as "... not dishonestly but purposely doing an act which the law forbids as tending to corrupt."

In R. v. Smith (John) [1960] 2 QB 423, 44 Cr. App. R. 55 CCA, it was held that although an appellant claimed to have offered a bribe for the purpose of exposing corruption, "corruptly" means with intention to corrupt and motive was irrelevant.

R. v. Kellam, ex parte South Wales Police Authority see Appendix 3.

Australian

The Queen v. Rogerson (1992) 174 CLR 268 FC 92/021 (1992) 60 A (Crim. R. 429).

Chapter 1

The Element of Moral Decay

In what is probably its most important aspect, corruption is decay in the physical sense, but in the kind of corruption with which this book is concerned, there is almost always an element of moral decay. However, let us put aside any question of biological dissolution and concentrate instead on the corrosive effect corruption has on the integrity of those who have a power which they are required to exercise. Bribery and corruption are criminal offences, punishable by fines or imprisonment. The law relating to the offences is relatively simple, being contained in two principal statutes which have been spared the huge weight of precedent or judge-made laws that can cling to legislation like barnacles. Even so, the legislation and discussion of the law has been relegated to an appendix for those who have more than a general interest in the topic and prefer not to delve into the textbooks.

A useful definition of bribery, culled from the *Oxford English Dictionary*, describes it as "A consideration voluntarily offered to corrupt a person and induce him to act in the interest of the giver". In the course of this book it may be of advantage to refer back to this simple statement to see whether or not it holds good in any particular circumstance.

The earliest of the statutes, The Public Bodies Corrupt Practices Act 1889, was enacted to deal with members, officers or servants of public bodies who receive or solicit something tangible or otherwise as an inducement to favour the other party. As an example - consider the council employee or agent who is responsible for receiving, and keeping secret, tenders for the purchase of local authority land, but reveals the bids of competitors to a land developer friend. The developer has clearly gained a valuable advantage over other bidders and, although the council has not suffered a financial disadvantage, both he and the council's employee would have some difficulty in persuading a jury that this was not corrupt.

The Prevention of Corruption Act 1906 was intended to deal with the agent who solicits or accepts an inducement to deal unlawfully with his principal's affairs and this was followed by the Prevention of Corruption Act 1916, intended to sweep up outstanding instances of corruption. All three statutes have been amended in so many respects that it is now difficult to separate the individual elements of each and the lines of demarcation have become blurred. It is perhaps worth making passing reference to the Honours (Prevention of Abuses) Act 1925, as an example of legislation aimed at preventing a particular form of corruption. The statute has nothing whatever to do with police corruption, but was enacted to deal with a glaring example of the misuse of power at the highest level of public service.

The awarding of Peerages and Baronetcies are within the gift of the Monarch. However, with the exception of awards for personal service, he or she will generally accept the advice of the Prime Minister. Just after the First World War, it was found necessary to curb the practice of Ministers selling honours by making their sale a criminal offence. There is presently an intention to introduce an all-embracing statute but one will have to await publication of the Bill, probably in early 2001. Although the prime purpose of this book is to look at police corruption - the problem, serious as it is, should be seen in perspective as only part of a widespread culture of corruption at many levels of public life.

When Sir Richard Mayne and Sir Charles Rowan became joint Commissioners of the newly formed Metropolitan Police in 1829, they had to decide what kind of men should be employed in the force. They adopted the course of recruiting those who, as far as it was possible to be certain, were honest men and were without criminal convictions to serve in the rank of constable. With the exception of a limited number of men who had served as Bow Street Runners or as parish constables, there was no pool of experienced people from which to select the best quality recruits. They had made up their minds that the New Police, as it was first known, would be a non-military body, provided with a civilian style of uniform consisting of a frock coat and top hat. Their intention in choosing this approach was to gain public acceptance of the constable's role as a civilian peace officer, rather than as a member of a kind of militia. They did not exclude former soldiers from membership, however, because such men brought with them the valuable quality of ingrained discipline. The engagement of former commissioned officers was quite a different matter. They were not particularly welcome.

Of the men who paraded to be sworn in on the first few days of the New Police, there remained only a small proportion on the first anniversary and by 1833, when the service had grown to over 3,000 men, only 562 of the first entrants were still serving. Most of those who failed to stay the course were dismissed for drunkenness, dishonesty or failing to meet the high standards set by the Commissioners. Dubious morality in connection with female relationships was a frequent charge, as was idleness or unpunctuality:

> "Constable Tucker was required to resign 'for ... that he took a lodging at the house of another Constable for a female and constantly visited her there ; also refused to give a satisfactory account of her respectability."
> "Constable Burden was dismissed for 'remaining in bed two hours after having been called, thereby preventing the ventilation of the bedroom; also being generally lazy in his habits."

Such were the Commissioners' views of morality and public image, that officers were expected to attend church each Sunday, in best uniform with white gloves, and accompanied by their families.

It was determined that with the exception of the rank of Sergeant, there would be no evidence of a military connotation through the names to be used in denoting other ranks; however, the very best men to hold the superior ranks were, in their view, former Sergeants and Sergeant Majors who had served in the Peninsular wars. It was from some candidates of their calibre that Sergeants, Inspectors and Superintendents were either appointed or promoted from the rank of constable. From the beginning, all promotions were to be made from the rank below and upon merit alone. Only two former commissioned officers were appointed but were found to be so unsuited to this unique employment that their tenure of office was brief. The Commissioners recognised the dangers of putting the new venture into the hands of men who had resigned their commissions, left the army for whatever reason, and might try to revive their military careers in a different uniform. For the most part, young men who wished to make a career of the army, bought their commission into whatever regiment their fathers could afford. History tells us that their bravery was rarely in question; however, their intelligence and ability to lead men was sometimes in doubt. By the very nature of the constable's duty, however rigid the discipline, he was obliged to use a degree of initiative when alone on his beat. Ex-officers of limited experience who had been accustomed to blind obedience from soldiers were unlikely to lead and inspire policemen.

Now, with the police established and feeling its way gently towards public acceptance, there began the first moves towards outside interference with the high ideals set by Mayne and Rowan by attempting to secure advantage from them by patronage. In his book, *British Police and the Democratic Ideal*, Mr Charles Reith reported that the Commissioners were subject to a torrent of requests to advance policemen by, among others, the Duke of Clarence, the Duke of Wellington, Lord Hill, Lord Fitzroy Somerset, the Speaker and some dozens of famous titled aristocrats. They were among the early recipients of the Commissioners' blunt refusals to comply. One of their written replies deserves quotation to illustrate the terse style of their refusal.

Whitehall Place
December 19, 1829

The Commissioners of Police present their compliments to Lord Melbourne and beg leave to acknowledge the receipt of his Lordship's letter in favour of John Kinham for promotion to the rank of Sergeant of Police.

The Commissioners will be glad to attend to his Lordship's wishes should it appear that this man is deserving of promotion.

* * *

That Lord Melbourne, described as a young man with the reputation of being a vapid and effete society lounger, would become Home Secretary and their immediate superior a year later, seems neither to have diverted them from their path nor troubled them in any way. The reader may care to consider whether or not such attempts at patronage may be described as corrupt in the purely moral sense. These aristocrats saw nothing wrong with trying to exert influence from positions of power on lesser mortals. Nor could they understand how their request, tantamount to an order, for the advancement of some favoured person, could be so rudely brushed aside. Complaints to Sir Robert Peel, the Home Secretary (and thus the Commissioners' immediate superior) were met with no better result. From the Commissioners' point of view, they were under a duty to administer an efficient service and a large part of that responsibility required that they selected the best people for the right jobs. Any attempt to divert them from the proper exercise of that duty, often by veiled threats, was wholly unacceptable and they refused to bow under them.

The first Commissioners had made their aspirations for the Metropolitan Police very clear. It was to be a body of men dedicated to serving the public bravely and fairly, as incorruptible and honest as humanly possible and which, in future years, would assist by advice and example in setting up police in every part of the country, based upon the same principles.

By 1850, Rowan had retired, leaving Mayne as the sole Commissioner, but by then it had been found advisable to form a small unit within the force to deal with major crimes such as murders, of which there were many. To this unit was appointed an Inspector called Charles Field, and a Sergeant, Jonathan Whicher. These two men, described as Detective Officers, soon made their mark in the roles assigned to them in dealing with most of the notorious crimes during the next few years. So successful were they that other officers were later brought in to augment their ranks. Field's background, although interesting in itself, is of little concern to this study, but he and Whicher were sufficiently well regarded that when the novelist and journalist, Charles Dickens, began to take an interest in the police in his writings, these were the men told to meet and assist him. He was allowed to go out with them on patrols to the poorest and most dangerous parts of London, where only men of Field's stature could survive unmolested. Field and Dickens struck up a good relationship and one can see the Detective reflected as a character in much of Dickens's literary work.

By 1860, a Detective department had become firmly established at Scotland Yard and its officers were sent to investigate serious crimes all over the country at the request of local Chief Constables. Field's days as a senior investigating officer had now come to an end upon his retirement from the police, but rather than sink into obscurity to live on his pension, he chose to set up a private inquiry agency in the Temple, professional home of London's lawyers. There was an abundance of lucrative work for private inquiry agents and Field was able to offer a high quality service based upon his experience. He was able to side-step much of the tedious work of the private Detective by calling on his former colleagues to keep him informed about matters of interest to him. This was a practice of dubious morality and presented some risk to those who passed confidential information to him, because to do so was an offence against good order and discipline for which dismissal was an inevitable consequence if found out. As a private citizen, no doubt Field did not regard his conduct in milking official sources of information as posing any kind risk to himself. He was to discover otherwise.

He took a partner in the business, a foreign national named Pollaky who had close contacts on the Continent where he was able to generate a lot of work with a British dimension in France and Holland. Private inquiry work was much more varied than that undertaken by modern practitioners, because the official police had limits upon the kind of inquiries they were permitted to undertake. To be a crime in police perception, the matter had to be clear cut with no suspicion that it might be a civil wrong, and the

Commissioner, ever alive to the cost of his police, did not want time wasted on anything that was not transparently police business. Circumstances which today would be regarded as clearly criminal, often fell into an uncertain area where the complainant would be obliged to employ lawyers and Private Detectives to help him obtain redress.

Field had been in private practice for some years and his earnings allowed him to improve his financial standing, supplemented by a useful pension from the force. His former colleagues began to hear unpleasant whispers suggesting that Field was misusing his former position as a retired officer to pursue private inquiries. Malicious whispers tend to drift high into the upper echelons and did so until reaching Commissioner Mayne's ears. Matters came to a head when Pollaky, engaged in investigating some action between parties living in England and Holland, wrote to the Dutch authorities in search of information. On August 17, 1861, policemen throughout London were able to read in that day's Orders, the following:

> Discontinuance of Pension
>
> "The Secretary of State for the Home Department has had his attention called to correspondence between the Police at Rotterdam and a person calling himself 'Superintendent du Department de l'Etranger' who dates his communication from the Foreign Department, Bureau de Surite, 20 Devereaux Court, which upon inquiry, is found to belong to Charles Frederick Field, late Inspector of the Detective Branch, Metropolitan Police. As no connection of any kind can be permitted to

exist between the Metropolitan Police and a person carrying on unauthorised practices, Sir George Gray has directed the Receiver [in effect, the treasurer] to discontinue the payment of the pension which was granted to Charles Frederick Field as a Superannuated Inspector of the Metropolitan Police."

Field appealed against this penalty, with abject apologies for this indiscretion which he attributed to Pollaky who had, he said, written the letter without his knowledge. The Home Secretary relented, restoring Field's pension in January 1862, on solemn assurances that Pollaky was no longer employed in the business, and that no more cause for complaint would occur. The following notice appeared in Police Orders.

Tuesday, January 7, 1862

Mr Field, late Inspector of the Metropolitan Police, the payment of whose superannuation allowance was stopped on account of his conduct in connection with a Private Inquiry Office, has given an assurance to the Secretary of State that no cause for the future shall be given for disapprobation, and that he will take steps at once to remove any impression that may exist that he acts in connection with the government.

Secretary Sir George Gray, in reliance upon these assurances, and in the full confidence that Field will regulate his future conduct in conformity with the promises he has made, has given directions to the Receiver to pay his pension as heretofore.

The matter of Field illustrates with great clarity the Commissioner's intention to maintain high standards of honesty, even among retired officers who might be tempted to act as Field did. In addition, there were many rumours that Field or his associate had paid serving officers for information helpful to their inquiries. There is no direct evidence that these rumours reached the Commissioner, but had they been proved accurate, it is unlikely that Field's pension would have been restored. Discipline was harsh and the punishment of taking away his pension was a serious blow, not only in financial terms, but also to his standing among police and lawyers. It must too, have had considerable impact upon those who knew Field personally, and on more than a few officers whose conduct, in the cold light of examination, was equally vulnerable. With the benefit of hindsight and history, the Commissioner's compassion in restoring Field's pension may be have been a serious error in that it minimised the seriousness of his offence in the eyes of his contemporaries and reduced the initial impact of the punishment. Had the discontinuance remained, the effect may have been *Pour encourager les autres* for many years: even being remembered until 1874, when senior Detectives were once more tempted ... and succumbed.

Of Mr Pollaky more will be heard when he had a walk-on part in the affair.

Chapter 2

The Promise of Easy Money

Betting has often been at the centre of much fraud for the obvious reason that it holds out a promise of easy money. There have always been professional gamblers who live on the proceeds of their gambling, but for the average player, wins are quickly followed by losses. Nevertheless they go on in the hope that, one day, three or four horses will each gallop home in first place to give them that elusive winning accumulator to make them rich. In pursuit of that dream, gamblers can be sitting targets for anyone who can offer them a fool-proof "system" bound to generate large winnings. To some involved in "the turf" there is a near certainty of making a very good living; these are bookmakers or as they prefer to describe themselves, Turf Accountants. The relationship between bookmaker and punter is an open and unambiguous one, because although the punter's risk of losing is very much higher, he at least goes in with wide open eyes. Others, smart operators with wonderful sales technique, can show handsome profits by defrauding foolish punters, rather than risking any of their own money on the uncertain outcome of racing.

From the Betting Act of 1853, until the introduction of the Betting and Gaming Act 1960, which allowed betting shops to be opened to the public, there was a distinct social difference between the working man and his betters in the way in which they were able to lay their bets. Whilst the first had uncertain access to the telephone, if at all, and had no account with a bookmaker in any event, the other could have had both a telephone and an account to be able to place his bets without breaking the law. The working man who wanted a little flutter, however, was obliged to rely upon the illegal "bookies runner" who, for a commission from the bookmaker, would lurk around street corners, public houses and factory gates to collect his customer's betting slips and money. The runner's main danger was from policemen in plain clothes who were wise to all possible dodges designed to escape arrest. Usually a Sergeant and two Constables, seconded from beat duty for a period of six months or so, would haunt the known collection spots and when they were sure that the runner had a pocket full of cash and slips, would take him before a magistrate who would impose a fine, often accompanied by a homily on the evils of gambling. The possibilities for corruption on a small scale were ever present in this situation and, for this reason, six months was regarded as the maximum time for which individuals should be engaged on the work. It was regarded as long enough for a team of officers to get to know the runners and their routine, but not long enough for them to fall into the temptation of turning a blind eye in exchange for a few pounds. As they were three in number, it was reasoned that a conspiracy would be difficult to operate without the willing participation of all of them. Street betting and its control had all the elements of a game played out by runners, bookmakers, police and magistrates as a matter of little real importance in the overall pattern of street life and offending.

It was as a result of horse race betting and the criminal elements who grafted themselves on to it, that a major scandal arose to cause serious damage to the Metropolitan Police in 1877, when four Senior Detective Officers were indicted at the Central Criminal Court for conspiracies and frauds. They represented a large part of the total men engaged at Scotland Yard in the Detective Branch, varying between eight and 12 at any one time.

The defendants, John Meiklejohn, Nathaniel Druscovitch, William Palmer and George Clarke were all Detective Officers, whilst a fifth defendant, Edward Froggatt, was a solicitor. The indictment in a criminal trial is intended to set out the precise offences with which defendants are charged: indictments in 1877 tended to be very long and detailed because at that time it was thought necessary to cover every possible element of the offence. The Indictments Act 1915 curbed this practice by insisting upon clarity and simplicity in charges, or counts as they are known. However, technical legal argument persists to this day about indictments which have been carelessly drawn or lack clarity, often resulting in an unjust acquittal. For those who might wish to study the indictment levelled against these men specimen counts from a total of 17 will be found in Appendix 1 but, for the purposes of the general reader, a brief summary of the allegations may well be more palatable.

The charges against the four officers, in essence alleged that they had assisted an organised gang of criminals to avoid justice by warning them of their impending arrest for betting frauds, and had been rewarded for doing so. Not all officers were charged in every count, some having joined the gang's schemes at different stages and, although this resulted in a cumbersome indictment, the jury's task was simplified by the Judge asking them at the end of his summing up to consider the conspiracy count alone. The jury retired to their room for less than an hour before returning to bring in a verdict of guilty on all but Chief Inspector Clarke. Reaction from the public gallery at this verdict was mixed and on reading the evidence in the case one can see that there were very good grounds to suspect that Clarke had been a rather lucky man. He had served in the police since 1840, first as a Constable, progressing in rank and prestige until the day of his arrest and charge. There is no doubt but that Clarke knew Charles Field, and must have known of his disgrace resulting from his activities with his partner Pollaky. He would have known, too, of the published change of heart by Authority. It is inconceivable that he did not know of Pollaky's activities as a Private Detective during the period 1870 to 1877, and who was at the very least on the fringe of the inquiries regarding Benson and the others.

Meiklejohn, during the dates covered by the charges was a Detective Sergeant, but by the time of his arrest he had been promoted Inspector. A man of 38, he had served for many years with some distinction.

Druscovitch held the rank of Detective Chief Inspector and was, at 37, another long-serving officer with an admirable record.

Palmer, too, was a Detective Chief Inspector aged 43 and second in command to Superintendent Williamson who held him in the highest esteem as an honest, intelligent and energetic colleague of many years standing.

Edward Frogatt was a young solicitor practising in and around Marlborough Street Police Court in central London and was well known in the courts as an enthusiastic and ambitious advocate. These then, were the remaining defendants in the case and it may be of interest at this stage to look at the co-conspirators some of whom were specifically named in the indictment as participants without being charged, because they had already been tried on substantive offences of fraud, convicted and sentenced to long terms of imprisonment. They were to be called as vital and willing witnesses for the Crown.

The first of the gang it was intended to call was Harry Benson who, in his opening address to the jury, the Attorney General described in the following terms:

> "He is the son of a very respectable merchant carrying on business in Paris. He is a man of excellent education. He is an accomplished linguist and, judging from what we know of him, an excellent scholar generally. He is a man apparently of great ingenuity and resource. I do not know if he has the boldness and determination of Kurr but if he has not perhaps he exceeds Kurr in adroitness, in subtlety and ingenuity. Benson was a British subject educated in France and partly in England. In 1872, he seems to have been in this country and in that year was engaged in perpetrating a fraud on the then Lord Mayor. I do not know if this was the first evil transaction in which he was employed. However that fraud was perpetrated. He was taken into custody, tried, convicted and sentenced to a year's imprisonment. He was confined in Newgate and the experience was distressing to him, for the unhappy position in which he found himself in; and the disgrace which had become upon him, and through him the very respectable family

apparently so affected and preyed upon his mind that he determined to commit suicide and attempted to so do by setting fire to the clothes of the bed on which he lay.

When he came out of prison in 1873 he (Benson) was a complete cripple. The lower part of his body was entirely paralysed and when he moved he was required to be carried. Benson became acquainted with William Kurr in 1874 apparently at that time or after he came out of prison until the autumn when he was endeavouring to gain an honest livelihood. So far as I can make out from the evidence, he had changed his name from Benson and assumed the name Young, though at times he went by other names. The way he became acquainted with Kurr was this - he advertised for employment of a literary character describing himself as a good linguist a person capable of making translations and writing for the newspapers upon many subjects; and that description he gave himself in the advertisement seems to have been perfectly justified. At this time, Kurr and those associated with him were carrying on, if not in the name of Phillip Gardner, some firm of a similar description in Scotland and it was necessary for them, in order to carry out their evil designs to defraud, not only the British but also the French public, and indeed the public generally, that they should have their circulars translated into a foreign language.

Kurr came into communication with Benson and employed him accordingly in preparing these papers for him. Soon a strong intimacy sprang up between Kurr and Benson, who forgot all his good resolution when he

> came out of prison and embarked, heart and soul with the rest of the gang in carrying out the schemes which they set on foot."

William Kurr was the leader of a gang which included his own brother, who were all actively engaged in a series of frauds. Most of the frauds were founded on the greed of those who were devoted to backing horses. He was the licensee of a public house, ran a small printing business and kept two race horses whom he named Chance and Coroner. A well-known figure at race meetings all over the country, he became known to Meiklejohn who frequented his public house and, on occasions met him at race meetings. It seems that they became friends. A Detective associating with a man whose activities were a little suspect would not, of itself be unusual either then or now, because such contacts can be one of the more valuable sources of information. Of course, such contacts must be carefully managed and the information gleaned subjected to very close examination. The informer's motive in letting slip some morsel of intelligence must be clear in the recipient's mind, because it is not unknown for a rival to ruin a competitor, even if the unfortunate target ends up in jail, guilty or not. In the course of his evidence at the trial Superintendent Williamson made it clear that this was an accepted practice in the Detective's work and he saw nothing inherently wrong in the technique, providing that the officer remained uncontaminated by the association. To accept money or any other gift from such a person would be wholly wrong and certainly an offence against the discipline codes. Indeed, even to borrow money from or lend money to a brother officer, was regarded as an extremely serious breach of discipline.

During the 20 days over which the Detectives' case was to be heard, Benson and Kurr would appear as Crown witnesses, entering the witness box dressed in the prison uniform of coarse woollen cloth stamped with prominent broad black arrows. Then, as now, it was recognised that a convicted criminal's evidence against an accomplice must be looked at with the utmost care, for he may have many reasons for going into the box. Revenge on a former friend perhaps, or acting on a promise of favours to come from the prosecution in the future. Less likely is that there has been a sudden attack of conscience, or a conversion on the road to Damascus. Whatever the motivation, providing that a clear warning is given to the jury about the possible danger of accepting an accomplice's evidence, it can be very persuasive and with the exception of Clarke, appears to have been so in all cases.

In about 1871, William Kurr was in the process of conducting frauds through the medium of companies set up and operating from rented accommodation. One of the companies operated in the name of Philip Gardner & Co., from Scotland; another in the name of the Discretionary Investment Society; another, this time in London, under the title Archer & Co., and the imaginatively named Society for Insuring against Losses on the Turf. Each of these organisations had the basic purpose of inducing gullible people to send money which would be "invested" on horse races in an infallible system on the forecast that their money would double and redouble in a short time. These sham companies were set up in short-term rented offices, with the operators using a variety of false names. Advertising in the sporting press brought cheques, cash and bank drafts tumbling in from the naive, who then sat back to await the promised profits. In due time, when nothing appeared, the by now suspicious punters went knocking on doors to inquire about the value of their "investments", only to find the office empty and the birds flown. Occasionally the plot was a more sophisticated one in which the punter was sent small cheques to represent fictitious winnings until his confidence in the company was built up. Then, when he had been lulled into a state of euphoria, requests for larger stakes would fall upon receptive ears. With a substantial amount of money safely tucked away and embarrassing inquiries about to burst upon them, the company and its directors would melt away, never to be seen again. It was something of the sort, although rather more elaborate, that required the assistance of Benson with his undoubted skills as a writer and translator; for their target was the wealthy Comtesse de Goncourt, a Parisian lady with a liking for playing the horses.

The de Goncourt fraud began with some inside knowledge of this lady's fascination with the turf. An attractive brochure was prepared, setting out the great successes of a new and totally secret method of making money on the race course, and Kurr arranged for a bogus newspaper, *The Sport*, to be printed and go out with the brochures. Every target selected by the gang received a brochure and copy No.1,713 of *The Sport*, in which the activities of Mr Montgomery, the paper's proprietor, were set out. It was claimed that this gentleman had been so successful in his system of selecting horses, and had won such large sums of money, that every bookmaker in England refused to accept any more bets from him. Mr Montgomery was therefore looking for sporting gentlemen and ladies who would be prepared to bet in their own names as his agent, using his money. The inducement was that he would pay a 5% commission on all his winning bets, at little inconvenience and absolutely no risk to the agents.

The Comtesse had been recommended, wrote Mr Montgomery in impeccable French, by the Franco-English Society of Publicity as a person whom he could trust, should the lady feel attracted to the offer, and he enclosed his personal cheque in the sum of £200 to demonstrate his confidence in her. She was simply asked to forward her own cheque in that sum to any one of Hugh Montgomery's London addresses, made out to a particular bookmaker nominated by Montgomery, who would then lay the bet in her name. When the horse won, as it must do under his system, he would send the bookmaker's cheque to her and in return, she would then send Montgomery another cheque drawn on her bank, after deducting her commission. There was a minor difficulty Montgomery explained, in that because all the cheques payable to her were drawn on the Royal Bank of London, they could not be lodged with her bank until the expiration of three months from the date of issue. This was necessary explained Montgomery, to comply with English law. The gullible woman did as she was asked, no doubt delighted to get her first commission with promises of more to come.

When Mr Montgomery sent her a cheque for £1,000, she readily wrote one for the same amount in the bookmaker's name and sent it him, tucking his cheque away until the law would permit her to bank it. Once again the system succeeded, so that she was able to note in her records a more substantial commission. After a number of similar transactions the time had come for Montgomery to spring the baited trap. He wrote to her in great confidence to say that his system had detected a positive golden opportunity which she should personally benefit from rather than continue their lucrative arrangement for a mere commission. It involved her raising the sum of £30,000 which should be sent to him in accordance with the usual arrangement but, with great generosity and some sacrifice to himself, he suggested that if she was unable to raise that sum, he would contribute half towards it. In 1873, a senior policeman was paid about £250 per annum in contrast to something in the order of £32,000 today [2001], so that using those sums as a basis for calculation it suggests that a sum in excess of £3 million was being asked of her. She sent him £10,000 in bills drawn upon various banks before approaching her financial advisers, instructing them to raise further funds from her investments. It was fortunate for her that there were no further readily available funds to draw upon and when her lawyer became aware of what she was doing, it took him very little time to discover the entire plot. He found that neither Mr Montgomery, alias Benson, nor the nominated bookmaker, had accounts with the Royal Bank of London for the simple reason that no such bank had ever existed; there was no law preventing her from lodging funds with a bank immediately; there was no such newspaper as *The*

Sport and the Comtesse was carefully preserving a packet of worthless forged cheques. The bookmaker for whose benefit she had drawn her cheques was Benson in one of his guises and he seemed to have had no difficulty in clearing her cheques through one of his bank accounts.

So confident were the gang that more money was coming from France and that a day or two more could do no harm, that they remained at the address to which she had been sending her money. In the meantime, her lawyers had tracked down one of her bills to a bank in Rotterdam and the Dutch police, having found an address for the gang, were actively seeking the men responsible.

Details of the fraud were reported to Superintendent Williamson and he ordered Meiklejohn and Druscovitch to go to the "bookmaker's" and arrest anyone found on the premises. He had quite rightly deduced that at least some of the gang would be there waiting for the lady's next contribution and, having got their hands on it would close the operation down, but he was becoming more and more certain that information was being leaked from his office in such a way that only a member of his staff could be responsible. There had been a number of occasions when a covert operation had gone wrong and the villains decamped, sometimes only minutes before officers had arrived to make an arrest. Someone was certainly leaking information to the Kurr gang, but he believed that security in the present case was so good that nothing could be let slip in time for the gang to escape. His confidence was misplaced because when the officers arrived at the premises, they found evidence of a very hasty departure and the premises empty. This debacle prompted Williamson to pass on his suspicions to the Commissioner and an investigation into the internal problems was conducted by a Treasury lawyer.

The friendship between Kurr and Meiklejohn had earlier developed into an unhealthy one. Kurr was very much better off than the policeman whose annual wage was in the region of £250 and, when Kurr treated him to meals and drinks on occasions when they chanced to meet at some race course, Meiklejohn probably did not consider it to be wrong. On the positive side Kurr was passing on useful information which allowed the officer to make a number of arrests, gaining him the kudos with which success is rewarded. However, in the course of conversations between them, there came a time when Kurr began looking for information and favours in return, reminding Meiklejohn of the help he had been given; in effect calling in the debt. Not enough is known at this time of Meiklejohn's character except that he had conducted himself well as a Detective until his involvement with Kurr. He was a married man with several children, and when he began receiving small sums of money from Kurr, the money was no doubt welcome. There is always a price to be paid for favours and the price was a deepening involvement in Kurr's web of fraudulent activities. As the gang's plan developed, Meiklejohn was introduced to the astute Mr Benson who very fully recognised the value of having a Scotland Yard officer compromised in the way that Meiklejohn had become. His chief value was in his ability and obligation to warn the gang of impending trouble from the police.

In 1874, during the currency of one of the frauds carried on under the cover of a firm called Archer & Co., Meiklejohn was assigned to the inquiry and, as it was put by the Attorney General during the trial, "It was his duty to expose them, but instead he gave energetic assistance and was paid the sum of £500 in cash, part of which he spent on buying a house". His value to the gang on this occasion was worth the equivalent of two years' wages. Then, having received either £100 or £150 pounds from Kurr as an insurance against arrest in connection with the Society for Insuring against Losses on the Turf, Meiklejohn was under an obligation to warn them if warrants of arrest had been issued against any of them. Warrants were issued and the gang received a telegram saying that "... the men should be ready to scamper out of the way". And scamper they did, for they knew from whom the telegram had come and precisely what it meant.

Every move that Williamson had made in his efforts to catch the gang were frustrated and it eventually became clear that among the officers in the Detective department, there was one or more involved in a conspiracy to defeat the ends of justice. The source of the leak was soon proved to be Meiklejohn who had begun the deterioration of a proud and efficient department, and the one who encouraged others to join in.

Druscovitch, or "the dustman" as he was nicknamed by Benson and Kurr, was deliberately drawn into the net by Meiklejohn. Druscovitch had been a police officer for many years and, like Meiklejohn, had a fine record of arresting criminals. He was a very good linguist, comfortable in

French and German at the very least and therefore a valuable asset to a department, much of whose work was international. He was introduced to Kurr by Meiklejohn in 1876 in the course of their normal duties and this first and quite proper contact was soon followed by more frequent meetings and, in all probability, the passage of useful information about criminals and their activities. If he had any doubts about Kurr when they first met, Meiklejohn's endorsement of the man settled any slight discomfort about their relationship, at least for the time being. Meiklejohn discovered that Druscovitch had a financial problem in that he had endorsed a bill for his brother which he could not now meet. The sum was a substantial one of £60 and he needed a loan to cover it in rather a hurry. The consequences of Druscovitch failing to pay on time could be devastating, for it was such a serious disciplinary offence to be in debt that the possibility of dismissal from the force was real if it should be discovered. Whether it was out of sympathy and friendship that Meiklejohn suggested helping, or to involve Druscovitch as a form of insurance against his discovering the true nature of what was going on, is unknown; however, Kurr must have been delighted to help and in due course he loaned Druscovitch the desperately needed £60. Later, and for no legitimate purpose, Kurr gave him a bag of 25 gold sovereigns and his involvement with the conspirators was sealed.

Druscovitch was assigned to the de Goncourt inquiry and appeared to be pursuing it with limited vigour. By now, there had been so many failures in the department, that Superintendent Williamson took every possible measure to prevent information about the progress of current inquiries reaching the criminals. It was to no avail because in many instances those who were carrying on not only this, but other frauds, were still being tipped off in good time. It had taken a long time and a good deal of heart searching before Williamson could admit to himself that there was corruption among his trusted subordinates and that the warnings were coming from one or more of them.

Chief Inspector Palmer was drawn into the net in a similar way and on Kurr's evidence, was said to have been paid sums of money to help the gang with information and timely warnings. There came into Superintendent Williamson's hands, an envelope containing among other things, a letter in Palmer's handwriting but signed W. Brown, and addressed to W. Gifford, one of Kurr's aliases. Reading between the lines it was a coded message that Druscovitch was on his way to the Isle of Wight where Benson, now a strong suspect, was living under the name of Young. A telegram in the same envelope carried the suggestion that Benson should decamp from the island at once, and an explanation would follow. There was also a piece of blotting paper on which in block letters were the words "keep the lame man out of the way", an obvious reference to the crippled Benson. There could be no innocent explanation for the contents of the documents and it was generally supposed that Kurr had sent these to Superintendent Williamson, perhaps to try to divert suspicion away from himself.

The solicitor, Froggatt, was an enthusiastic and energetic member of the gang's supporters. His hand can been seen in many aspects of the conspiracy, but particularly in attempts to interfere with the proper lawful process. For example, there came a time during the closing stages of the de Goncourt swindle when Benson and others had scampered to the Netherlands, but had been arrested by the Rotterdam Police and imprisoned whilst awaiting extradition to England. Froggatt concocted a telegram, purporting to have come from Superintendent Williamson and addressed to the chief officer in Rotterdam, stating that the men in custody were not those wanted by Williamson, and asking that they be released at once. A letter in confirmation was to follow. The Rotterdam police did not fall for this somewhat amateurish ploy but checked with Williamson by telegraph. The defendants were handed over to an escort from London, headed by Druscovitch and whilst there is no way in which one can discover what passed between them during the voyage back to England, one imagines that the conversations would have been most interesting.

It was the de Goncourt fraud that finally put an end to the Detectives' criminal conduct because, on the gang's return from Rotterdam, and after their conviction and sentence, they offered to tell the whole story and give evidence against their former protectors.

William Kurr was the first prosecution witness to be called in the trial and his story was devastating. He said that he knew Meiklejohn as a police officer, having spoken to him on a number of occasions about betting and the dishonesty that was rife among the betting fraternity and those running various dishonest schemes. Kurr, at that time, was running the dishonest Phillip Gardner enterprise in Scotland, and when he saw Meiklejohn in a pub in London, the officer showed him a police handbill concerning the current swindle. Meiklejohn knew that the Scottish enterprise was Kurr's and both knew that some very speedy movement was necessary before disaster struck them. Meiklejohn explained that when he next saw Kurr he would be obliged to arrest and charge him with the fraud and, to avoid this, it was decided that Kurr would decamp to America for a short time.

Another of the gang, a man named Eustace, was arrested for the fraud which had, in the event, proved to be unprofitable. On Kurr's return to England he met Meiklejohn again and, referring to Eustace and the Phillip Gardner affair, Meiklejohn said, "I can fix that for you for a 100 quid". Kurr told the jury that he had paid Meiklejohn the 100 pounds and nothing further was heard of the affair so far as he was concerned. The case against Eustace was duly withdrawn and it is highly probable that Meiklejohn had exerted some influence with an official at Bow Street Police Court, or interfered with the matter in some other way to frustrate a trial.

There came a stage in Kurr's evidence when he told the court that he had met Druscovitch and told him of his plans to open a private betting office for people living in France to place bets in England.

> Druscovitch asked, "is it a legitimate affair" and I replied "yes". I asked him to let me know when any applications were made for warrants or any complaints lodged. He said "what is the name?" to which I replied, " Montgomery". I said, "Here is £25 for you" and I gave him the money in gold coins in a little bag. He said,

> "Oh! I already owe you something" and, "How am I to communicate with you if anything turns up", he afterwards said, "I will write to you in such a way that nobody will understand it apart from ourselves". He went on to say in evidence he had seen Druscovitch outside the back of Scotland Yard, who told him that a big swindle had come in from Paris. "I said, is it a racing affair?" and he said, "No I don't think so - it has something to do with spurious bills of exchange." He added that a solicitor had been to the office about it. I said, "Keep the case in your hands". He said "It's all right, I have all the papers in my files".

A few days later they met again and Druscovitch said, "I have been piped off", which Kurr understood him to mean that he was being followed or watched by another Detective. "I did not, however believe him at the time". There was then some other conversation and then he walked away very sharply. He said, " I have told you now and you will have to look out for yourself". Next day I saw Meiklejohn in Derby, I said, "There is something turned up and you must come to London and see Druscovitch". I told him we had been receiving a lot of money from France. Meiklejohn asked if I had seen Druscovitch and I said that I had but had no information from him. I got all the news from the old man, meaning Chief Inspector Clarke. He said, "We have to do all this work directly the stink comes. How did the old man take it, did he funk it at all?" I said, "Yes, he did. He called my attention to the fact of our leaving places suddenly. I suppose you have left all the joints, meaning all the offices where the swindle was carried out". I said "Don't you think Mr Williamson will be suspicious about this?" to which Meiklejohn said, "He's a calf. He will never tumble to it for a thousand years," and laughed. I saw Druscovitch when his train came into the station at Derby, and the conversation referred to the letters written in French to Madam de Goncourt. "Druscovitch", I said, " have you got any warrants out?" Druscovitch said, "Yes, we have got them out today". I asked who had issued the warrants and he said, "Mr Knox [one of the magistrates] I suppose you'll go to America now". I said, "No" and he said, "I must arrest somebody over this lot."

Kurr, in continuing his evidence, related how they discussed how they could continue the betting business without getting caught and was advised of a number of places where, because Druscovitch knew the local police officer, it would be safe to start up again. If his story is to be believed, he had been bribing police officers all over the country, and even had the clerk at Marlborough Street Police Court in his pocket. One attempt to put off a witness who might be willing to identify him in an incrimination situation was revealed in this exchange between himself and Froggatt when he suggested that he "... Tell Flintoff to say that he had made a mistake that night. That the light was bad and that his identification of me [Kurr] was wrong". Froggatt reported back that he had seen Flintoff and offered him 50 quid to change his evidence, reminding him that "You were a brother Mason". Flintoff would not agree to do this but remarked that if he can't do you any good, he would not do you any harm.

Another witness in Kurr's own trial, a potman at the Northumberland Hotel who was able to identify Kurr in compromising circumstances, was seen by Froggatt who reported back that he had offered the man a fiver and he agreed not to identify Kurr in court. At the end of Kurr's evidence he had shown himself to be totally dishonest in every respect, nevertheless none of the very experienced defence counsel could shake him by cross-examination to any significant extent. His evidence in respect of Clarke was particularly damaging but, perhaps it was because the Chief Inspector was so well respected that even the Commissioner of Police gave evidence of his good character, that the jury acquitted him, on the face of it against the weight of the evidence. With regard to the other defendants his evidence signalled the end for them.

As an interesting aside, the defendants did not give evidence in their own defence because the law as it then was did not allow it. Any defence they were able to put up had to come from the mouths of prosecution witnesses under cross-examination, or from witnesses called by themselves to contradict the prosecution case. The reasoning behind the prohibition was that a man under pressure of prosecution in earlier times, when conviction of relatively minor crimes could result in his execution, was under too great a temptation to lie on oath. It was thought unjust to put a defendant under that awful burden in the interests of his mortal soul, for it was thought better for him to suffer the extreme penalty of the law than be consigned to hell-fire and damnation for taking the Lord's name in vain. The disability was not necessarily a bad thing, however, because it is within the experience of most lawyers today that the solemn oath is often considered to be merely a form of words to be gabbled through as quickly as possible, and as quickly forgotten. More importantly, the effect of defendants giving evidence on their own behalf is that they must face cross-examination, and it is at that point where carefully crafted defences which sounded so good in their lawyer's office often crumble into dust.

Benson was called to give evidence on October 30, 1877, and on that day *The Times* published a review of an article which had appeared in the French newspaper *Figaro.* It read:

> "At Brussels during the war of 1870-71 the author of this account made the acquaintance of Benson at the house of a common friend. The notorious swindler was then a young man of about 23: slightly built but with an expression of energy, and he went by the simple name of M. Benson. This humble cognomen, however, people said, intended to conceal the scion of a noble race, his real title being Comte de Montegut (Montague), son of a General of Division. If, for the moment, he chose to call himself Benson, this was merely with a view of not casting a blot on the family coat of arms, circumstances having imposed on him the dire necessity of gaining a livelihood by contributing to a newspaper. The contributor to *Figaro,* in [his] confiding moments, expressed some surprise that a young man bearing so noble a name and the son of a General of Division, should be spending his time at Brussels playing cards, while his proper place was in France by the side of his soldier father; but the Comte de Montegut was ready

with a triumphant reply, the fact being that he was high in favour with the Imperial family, and had chosen Brussels as a place to dwell in, merely that when the moment came, he might serve as a bond of union between France and the banished Empress.

The Count made frequent visits to London, and always on returning, assumed mysterious airs. He was so well pleased with Belgium that he resolved to continue to live there. He therefore bought a fine mansion, started horses and carriages and became a man of consequence and fashion. For some weeks, indeed, the town talked of nothing but the dashing Comte de Montegut. One fine morning, however, the noble dandy was arrested, and the secret of his extravagance was revealed. Towards the end of the war he had provided himself with false letters of introduction to the Lord Mayor of London, as a mendicant envoy from the town of Chateaudun, in France. The unfortunate place had suffered most fearfully in the war and stood in crying need of succour. Softened by the harrowing story of Benson's, the Lord Mayor did not think twice. He made the ambassador of Chateaudun stay to dinner, and over the walnuts and wine handed him a cheque for 50,000 francs, out of the War Victims Relief Fund, begging him at the same time to express to the citizens of Chateaudun, the hearty sympathy of the City of London. Put upon his track at last, the police succeeded in capturing the delegated suppliant in full career of squandering his money abroad. There followed extradition, trial and imprisonment."

This then was the man who stepped into the witness box in his prison uniform to drive home the stories given by William Kurr. This too, was the man who had completed the corruption of the Detectives. He told of meetings with the Detectives; of false names and cryptic letters; and of sums of money handed over to them and in particular to Chief Inspector Clarke. Of one thing there can be no doubt, that Benson, young as he was, stood head and shoulders above the defendants, in both intellect and in native cunning. Clarke had written a letter to one of the conspirators in which it was possible to interpret as revealing some dishonesty in the way he was dealing with them. Benson made good use of this letter and it was not long before Clarke was being subjected to "suggestions" about the uses to which it could be put, and the price to be paid for not falling in with those suggestions. Clarke, foolishly, did not report the problem to Williamson, but tried to deal with the implied threats on his own. He wrote a number of letters to Benson who was then living on the Isle of Wight in the name of Young or Yonge, asking that his first letter be returned to him and that the subsequent letters be returned or destroyed. They were far too valuable to Benson and his team to be returned, far less destroyed, and therefore they were kept as an insurance against Clarke screwing up the courage to report the whole sorry mess to his superiors. With such material in their hands, would not the rogues make use of it? Benson's letters to Clarke were cryptic but supposedly clear to the recipient; however they were not in Benson's own handwriting, but that of a servant who copied his letters for him. One letter from Benson to Clarke concerning the letter he was trying so hard to recover, read "Dear Sir and Brother, we exchanged promises at our last meeting, yours was that you would give me an early opportunity of proving our friendship, mine that I would show you how kindly I feel towards you". The letter went on to say that he had some information for Clarke who should come down immediately. Clarke replied with the same form of address, namely "... My dear Sir and Brother ..."

The Attorney General pointed out that this form of address was used because the two men were Freemasons. Freemasonry was raised again during the evidence of Flintoff who said that he had been called as a witness in the magistrates' court against Kurr. "At the police court, Froggatt told me that Kurr was a good fellow, adding that he was a Freemason and in distress. He then asked me to help him." At this stage the judge asked Flintoff if he was a Mason, to which he agreed that he was. "I told him that Freemasonry was not intended to assist persons of that description and that I wanted nothing more to do with the matter. Froggatt said that he had instructed a Mr Lewis to defend Kurr, and that I should go to him and tell him that I could not identify him. For this I would be given £50. I did not do so."

When asked how he knew Froggatt, Flintoff described having seen him for the first time in the street shortly before the court case and, having been given a Masonic sign by Froggatt, was bound to speak to him. Brotherly love appears to have dried up somewhat after this brief acquaintance, because Froggatt drew a summons against Flintoff claiming that he had given perjured evidence in the case. This ploy failed.

The Attorney General seems to have had Freemasonry within his sights, because he called as a witness, the secretary of a Masonic Lodge to give evidence about a meeting of the lodge and who produced an attendance book showing that Clarke and Palmer had attended, with Palmer occupying the chair of Junior Warden. The object of calling this evidence appears to be that the Crown wanted to show a connection between the two men on that particular date and, perhaps, to show that there was a bond between them in their membership of the lodge that might conflict with their duty as police officers.

Before leaving the evidence in this case, it will be interesting to revisit Mr Pollaky whose activities have been mentioned in connection with former Inspector Field. Detective Sergeant Riemers was called to give evidence about conversations between himself and Druscovitch, details of which showed how deeply Druscovitch was involved with the gang. He was cross-examined by Mr Straight, counsel for Druscovitch, and it was suggested to him that there had been many complaints about him and the way in which he had performed his duties. This Riemers denied, but agreed that he had been prosecuted for assault "... Yes, when you prosecuted me and failed to get a conviction [laughter in court]."

"You were an Inspector at one time I believe ?"

"Yes, I was reduced to the position of Sergeant on December 24, 1876. It was alleged by Mr Pollaky who was instigated by Druscovitch, that I had furnished him with a rough draft of my Bremerhaven report (this had no connection with the trial but was part of an attack upon the officer's integrity)".

"Was it not alleged that you gave information to Pollaky who is a private inquiry agent?"

"It was alleged".

"Were you at one time friendly with this man Pollaky?"

"Yes".

"And in December last, for some reasons between yourselves you quarrelled?"

"No, we were good friends".

"Then your story is that Druscovitch set Pollaky to inform against you?"

"Yes, that is it. I allege that there was a conspiracy between Druscovitch and Pollaky to ruin me".

Various witnesses were called on behalf of the defendants, but the sum total of their evidence was merely to underline the previous good character and valuable services carried out by the Detectives. The Attorney General and defence counsel all had their final speeches and Baron Pollack summed up the case for the jury. They returned their verdicts in under an hour and it is interesting to observe that they recommended that Druscovitch and Palmer be dealt with leniently but added no such rider to their verdicts on Meiklejohn and Froggatt.

On announcing the verdict of "not guilty" in Clarke's case, there were, "Cheers mingled with some manifestations of disapproval". As soon as the guilty men had made their own impassioned plea for leniency, Baron Pollack passed a sentence of two years' imprisonment and to be kept to hard labour. He considered that the breach of trust in each case was so serious that only the maximum sentence was appropriate, and expressed his view that the law should be changed to allow heavier sentences in such cases.

At Scotland Yard there remained of the once proud and respected Detective Department, only a few Sergeants and Superintendent Williamson. Chief Inspector Clarke, although acquitted and having had his salary and pension rights restored, was quietly ushered out of the service within a few weeks on voluntary retirement.

What had gone wrong?

Perhaps the nature of the Detectives' work was such that close supervision was not possible? Perhaps the trust built up between Williamson and his men over many years had blinded him to the possibility of their being corruptible? Did their membership of a Masonic lodge create bonds of loyalty between the defendants, stronger than the shackles of duty? Some of them would have known, or at least heard of, the legendary Inspector Field, his disgrace and rehabilitation. Was it, therefore, a mistake on the part of the Commissioner and Secretary of State to create a precedent by allowing Field to be publicly reinstated to his former standing instead of remaining a disgraced marker for others to note? Financial need should not have been a motive for the conspiracy, because two of the officers were near the top of the police hierarchy with a good standard of income for the times. It might be argued that Meiklejohn was the bad apple which began the rot, an excuse trotted out with great regularity in modern times by senior officers when their men have gone wrong. Whilst there is some attraction in the idea, it is too facile an excuse to disguise poor selection of manpower and inadequate supervision of vulnerable staff.

It was a long time before the Detective Department regained anything like its former standing with the public, so that honest, brave and hard-working officers must have felt diminished by the events. In a little under a 100 years conditions were ripe for another major upheaval, this time of even greater dimensions.

Chapter 3

Aftermath of the Meiklejohn Scandal

Little is known of developments within the police following the Meiklejohn scandal, or of the means by which the Detective Department regained public confidence. One can assume that increased supervision, coupled with the knowledge that Detectives who fell into crime could easily find themselves in prison, probably discouraged others from following that path, at least for a time. However, new generations of officers would have heard less and less of it as time passed, and those who were inclined to dishonesty would be undeterred by events of long ago. One thing is certainly clear; that all the myths and mysteries surrounding the CID slowly but surely helped in building it into an autonomous part of the Metropolitan Police, governed by its own senior officers and, although strictly speaking under the Commissioner's command, a law unto itself.

By 1895, the Criminal Investigation Department had been operating under that name for a number of years and even then was known among its members as "the department" an abbreviation still in use today. In that year, a man who was to become Chief Constable of the CID at Scotland Yard, Frederick Porter Wensley, joined the department, having served his spell in uniform first at Lambeth. In his autobiography one can see how the CID had begun to seize the public interest with Detectives and their work, fuelled by highly detailed press reports of notorious crimes together with outpourings of crime novelists. With this public exposure, it is hardly surprising that many officers fell into the habit of aping their fictional counterparts and became caught up in a personality cult. To the law-abiding, the Detective was a charismatic figure fighting crime with courage and resource, but to the criminal he was someone to be feared. It seems likely that the public, if they remembered the problems more than 20 years earlier, now regarded the police service as a reputable organisation in which they could place their trust.

In 1916, when Detective Inspector Alfred Ward, the Senior Detective at Scotland Yard was killed by a Zeppelin bomb, Wensley took over the small group of Senior Detectives who seemed to delight in being called *The Big Four* by the press. A contemporary photograph of these officers shows a group of impeccably dressed, suave, self-confident men whose very appearance invited admiration and public respect. Wensley found that Senior Detectives on each division, were reluctant to allow their men to make inquiries outside their own area, and, conversely, discouraged outsiders from entering their's. This parochial attitude made little sense to Wensley and he gradually introduced integration between the divisions. He also realised that there should be a central unit capable of giving help to the divisions and being sufficiently mobile to provide that assistance quickly. As a result, a small body of men was organised to pursue coiners in whatever part of the Metropolis they were operating. As an experiment it was not a resounding success and it was some years before a similar scheme was created to deal with all kinds of crime, this time with much better results. The germ of an idea, later be put into effect and called by the press the "flying squad", began to germinate. During Wensley's service there seems to have been relatively few complaints of corruption made against the CID and its reputation remained high.

By 1929, when Wensley retired, he was able to look back on a department which had expanded to meet the demands of the time and to have changed in its composition and thinking.

On November 29, 1969, *The Times* newspaper published an article in which it was alleged that three Detectives of the Metropolitan Police had been taking bribes in exchange for dropping charges against a known criminal, playing down the seriousness of certain evidence offered in court, and allowing him to work unhindered. These allegations proved to be the forerunner of a catalogue of corruption scandals of even greater dimensions than those of 1877. To help set the scene and gain some understanding of how the situation could have developed, it may be interesting to look at the post-war set-up of the London CID, how its staff was recruited and the environment in which it was obliged to operate. What follows is in a large measure my personal experience and perception during a period beginning in 1952, in "N" Division, covering Holloway, Highbury Vale, Stoke Newington and Kentish Town, and continuing until about 18 months later when my discomfort with the situation led me to transfer into a Home Counties service.

In 1948, upon joining the Metropolitan Police, I found that the majority of recruits in that month's intake were men and women who had served in one of the armed forces. The exceptions were a few from the newly disbanded Palestine Police with an automatic right of entry under what would now be termed a redundancy package, and a number of Irish nationals without military or police experience. Of the ex-service recruits, many had held wartime commissions whilst, of the remainder, none had held a rank lower than Sergeant or its equivalent. At the expiry of some 10 weeks' basic police training at Peel House in London, each Probationary Constable was posted to a Division where training continued in various ways including a month patrolling beats with an experienced Constable whose task was to ease the new boy (or girl) into the realities of day-to-day police work. After about a month, the newly fledged officer was posted to a beat and expected to act on his own, having considerable discretion to exercise all the considerable powers attached to his position as an officer under the Crown. It was drummed into recruits at the training school that the Constable was at the most important level of policing, and that those who served in that rank were the élite of the police service. Few accepted this piece of propaganda in spite of its inherent truth, and those with ambition preferred to believe that there were more attractive areas of work in one of the specialist departments after a suitable period passed on the beat. An interesting view was expressed to the group by a representative of the Police Federation, a hoary old Constable who served as one of the senior members of that well-intentioned but largely toothless watchdog. His firm opinion was that if a member of the public spoke to a policeman on his beat, then he wanted something. Senior officers were only concerned with their own interests he claimed, and not those of the Constables. The only remedy was that each of us should watch his or her colleague's back and it is in the light of this entrenched philosophy that what later became known as the "canteen culture" existed.

There were a limited number of those specialist

opportunities in units such as traffic patrols, river police, and the mounted branch, but the largest department was the Criminal Investigation Department. The CID had a certain glamour about it with the result that there was always a large pool of volunteers anxious to enter its ranks. It was a simple matter of making a written request for consideration and waiting until the piece of paper had made its way across the desks of numerous supervisory officers until it arrived at that of the Detective Chief Inspector.

Having been selected for a trial on the path to becoming a Detective, the officer put his uniform away and took to the streets in plain clothes with the simple instruction to go out and catch thieves. Each new hopeful, described as an "Aide to CID", was attached to an experienced man, usually one who had no real ambition to go further, but was content with the freedom his job allowed him. They were men with many years' experience of low level crime and criminals, who were well able to teach the elements of finding, recognising and arresting them. One of the most fruitful sources of arrests were in areas which had suffered bomb damage and from where scrap metal, particularly lead, could be spirited away to the nearest scrapyard. In the immediate post-war period, non-ferrous metals fetched a good price from scrap metal dealers where questions were seldom asked. Most of the arrests were of men struggling under the weight of a roll of old lead sheet, en route to the dealer's yard. Or a better equipped young villain pushing an old pram loaded with a coil of lead water pipe. In most cases the prisoner would offer some half-hearted story, be arrested, charged, and taken before a magistrate next morning to be awarded three months or so in jail.

Another source of arrests was opened up by the stop and search provisions contained in the Metropolitan Police Act. It was enough for a constable to have a suspicion that someone was in possession of property stolen or unlawfully obtained to be entitled to stop and search them and it was surprising to discover what a wide variety of illegally acquired property was being carried about the streets. Each month a list was posted in the CID office, to show against the name of each Detective or aide the number of arrests he had made. To have a blank space against one's name as an aide was excused once or twice, but any further default resulted in a rapid return to the uniformed beat and a sad farewell to the chance of becoming a Detective. That was not the end of matters, even for an aide who achieved a satisfactory number of arrests, because the kind of crime for which he was making arrests was important too. There had existed, almost since the force's beginning, an offence of "being a suspected person, loitering with intent to commit a felony". In recent years, what had come to be known as the "suss" law was repealed following the exposure of numerous cases of injustice, usually as the result of allegedly perjured evidence given by aides to CID. The law was simplicity itself in that in order to prove that a person was loitering with intent to commit a felony, the arresting officer must first see an act which raised his suspicion that a crime might be committed, for example the suspect trying a door handle of a parked car. Then there must be a further "overt act" as it was termed, such as trying another car door. The evidence of two such connected acts was usually sufficient for the court to convict on the premise that the first act rendered the prisoner a suspect and the second confirmed the initial suspicion. From there it was a short step to accept that two such acts were good evidence of an intention to commit a felony. Such incidents did in fact happen, and many arrests were made of people whose intention was to steal from a car, or perhaps walk into a school or office to take handbags from a staff room. However, there were very many "suss" arrests made simply to provide a necessary entry on to the monthly score sheet. It required no more than two frustrated but ambitious aides, spotting a known minor criminal in an area where there might be something to steal, for them to conjure up two overt acts embellished with evidence of his furtive looks to guarantee his conviction.

When an aide was unable to show arrests of suspected persons, his explanation was closely examined by the Senior Detective Officer in the Division and, if the reason was an unwillingness to conform to the pattern, the officer was considered to lack moral fibre. It was most unusual that such an officer would progress in the CID in those circumstances unless his arrest record for genuine crimes was exceptional or he possessed some special quality. Otherwise the almost inevitable result was a return to uniformed duties.

It must be said that injustice of this kind was usually meted out to young villains whom the officer knew, with a degree of certainty, were habitually getting away with petty crimes and who therefore accepted being arrested as a "suss" without too much ill-feeling. In recent years, following some notorious incidents of policemen lying on oath, a senior police officer coined the phrase "Noble cause perjury", presumably intending this to mean that the actions of a police officer who has lied to prevent the improper acquittal of a guilty person may be understood, if not entirely excused. The damage to public trust in the police when officers are caught out telling lies under oath is very great and should dispel any notion that "noble cause perjury" may somehow be acceptable. When considering the many Detectives who were involved in the "Firm within a firm" case and subsequent revelations it will be well to remember that most, if not all, began their CID careers in the same atmosphere and under the same pressures.

The aide system came to an end, at least in name, in 1963/4 following a notorious case of deliberate perjury in an attempt to pervert the course of justice.

During the evening of July 11, 1963, the King and Queen of Greece were staying at Claridges Hotel in Brook Street, London, a visit which sparked off a demonstration by Greek activists against them. In the course of the evening a number of young people were arrested and charged with public order offences, allegedly in connection with the demonstration. The evidence against two of them was statements made by three aides to CID, who planted pieces of brick on the defendants and supported the charges with perjured evidence. In control of the aides that evening was a Detective Sergeant Challoner. In 1964, the three aides were convicted at the Central Criminal Court of conspiring with Challoner to pervert the course of justice by making unlawful arrests, making false statements and by fabricating evidence.

In passing sentence Mr Justice Lawton said, "The mere

recital of the facts shows what a terrible crime you committed. Honest police officers are the buttresses of society. Dishonest, perjured police officers are like an infernal machine ticking away to the destruction of us all. I take into consideration that you were working possibly under the direction and certainly under the supervision of a Detective Sergeant who, I am satisfied at the material time, was mentally unbalanced, but you must have known perfectly well that you were doing the gravest wrong". The three officers were sentenced to imprisonment ranging from four to three years, whereas Challoner was found to be insane and unfit to plead. Victor Durand, QC, counsel for the three officers, told the Judge that Challoner was a forceful character and it was not improper to describe him as a tyrant. They may not have liked to stand up to Challoner and once having taken the first step it was impossible for them to extricate themselves.

By 1969, Meiklejohn and his brother officers had been long forgotten and Wensley's innovations had found their place in the CID organisation. Now at its head was an Assistant Commissioner (Crime), answerable only to the Commissioners whilst below him there were Commanders, Chief Superintendents, Chief Inspectors, Sergeants and Constables. Of these, 3,200 male and female officers were stationed within 23 divisions, grouped around police stations from Bushey in Hertfordshire, to St Mary Cray in Kent. The remainder served in one or other of the specialist units at Scotland Yard, later to be renamed New Scotland Yard when the new headquarters was opened in Victoria Street. The department was run by its senior officers who had the duties of discipline, management and promotion. It wanted no outside influences to mar the self-satisfied organisation it had become, nor did elements of the department want critical eyes being cast on the members' practices. Consider, for example, how difficult it would be for a senior officer to discipline a Junior Detective, caught out in a lie at court or some other disreputable act, when he himself was known to be guilty of the same kind of thing. With discipline being a matter entirely within the department's responsibility, such difficulties could be overcome and usually dealt with by a caution to be more careful in the future. On those occasions when a formal complaint was made against a Detective, a Senior Detective was put in charge of the inquiry. If the Detective subject of the complaint had the support of his superiors for whatever reason, and it was possible to do so, the investigation could be structured towards vindication. It was for these reasons that in spite of a steady flow of complaints of corruption, they rarely resulted in a Detective being disciplined and even more rarely being brought before a court. It was also for these reasons that there developed an arrogance among many based upon the certainty that what they were doing was justified and would be seen as such by their contemporaries. It would be most unfair to suggest that all members of the CID were part of this culture because a significant number distanced themselves from it, conducting their investigations honestly to achieve just results. Unhappily, as events were to prove, there were far too few of that kind.

It was under this protective shell that the new member of the CID found him or herself, and soon became accustomed to, a well developed supportive camaraderie. On appointment as a Detective Constable, his whole method of working changed. He no longer had to patrol the streets in the hope of picking up minor criminals engaged in their small crimes, but became fully employed in investigating reported crimes. Investigation followed the usual routine of attending the scene, looking for physical traces such as foot- and fingerprints, blood stains, weapons and a whole range of items that might throw up a suspect who could then be questioned. In a large proportion of crimes, the suspect is obvious and the task of proving his guilt can be tackled with whatever resources are available including interrogation or the careful assembling of evidence. However, when there is no obvious suspect, the Detective must attempt to draw up a list of possibles from local knowledge, from *modus operandi* or by whispers from an informer with some axe to grind. Without a stable of informers, a Detective was of limited effectiveness, so that on appointment to the CID he was encouraged to form a personal bond with those on whom he could call when needed.

The life of an informer can be hazardous and before a man engages himself in it there must be a strong incentive to take the risk of becoming recognised as such among his contemporaries. Of the many reasons for informing, money takes first place with guarantees of immunity from prosecution as an important subsidiary temptation; in essence to be given a licence to steal and rob. It is only afterwards when the informer is thoroughly compromised that his motives may change to fear of exposure as a "grass" if his supply of reliable information should happen to dry up. In a word, through blackmail.

The cultivation and motivation of informers is, by any standards, a pretty murky business and it should be no surprise to find that Detectives who are obliged to call on their services can become ruthless in their recruitment and use of them. The extensive employment of informers was a normal, regular activity of the officers who will be mentioned in connection with many of the corruption inquiries, in common with entirely honest Detectives who stay on the right side of the fence.

The availability of substantial funds is necessary to attract high quality information and it is in this connection that temptation can so readily arise. Before the massive cleansing of the CID's Augean stables in the wake of the scandals, it was common practice for officers who had been successful in recovering stolen property, to obtain the standard reward of 10% of the value from insurance companies who had held the stock at risk. Insurers would not, of course, reward officers for doing their duty but were content to pay for the efforts of a police informer in recovering their goods. There was many a frightened minor thief who found himself taken into the presence of an insurance company representative by a couple of Detectives, to collect a large cash reward with no questions asked and no receipts given. The "informer" was then encouraged to hand over the reward, accept a small sum for his trouble and advised to keep his mouth shut. The remainder was available to be disbursed at the discretion of the officers involved. Whilst it can be assumed that some of the reward money was used to further the cause of public good by paying off genuine informers, the temptation to dishonesty was often irresistible. There was an element of control by Senior Detectives of course but the relationship between an officer and his informer was considered sacrosanct; a relationship not to be disturbed by a meddling superior without good reason. Detectives of all ranks regarded the confidentiality of that relationship in much the same light as the journalist's refusal to disclose his source; the priest's to reveal his penitent's secrets and the doctor his patient's condition. However, should it happen that the informer becomes an embarrassment for some reason he can easily be thrown to the wolves, for loyalty between officers and their "snouts", as they are often called, is a fragile thing. The following example illustrates the kind of difficulties that can sometimes arise.

In recent years the writer had experience, as defence counsel, of attending a Crown Court with instructions to represent a man charged with possessing drugs of Class A with intent to supply to another, a crime carrying a high risk of lengthy imprisonment. The brief was delivered late on a Friday evening for trial on the next Monday morning and, in spite of the short notice, appeared to contain all the information necessary to conduct the trial subject to having a satisfactory conference with the defendant on the morning of the court. As one might accept, it is not always possible to contact instructing solicitors during their jealously guarded weekends.

The prosecution case was that the defendant had been seen by uniformed officers in the street late one night, to pass some Ecstasy tablets to another man and receive cash in exchange. He was arrested and taken to a police station.

There he asked to speak to a named officer of the Drugs Squad, claiming that when arrested he was actually engaged on a sting operation for that officer for whom he was a valued informer. The Drugs Squad officer came to the station, spoke to him and against all the odds in a situation of this kind, arranged for him to be released on bail pending further inquiries. When the defendant returned to the police station some weeks later, contrary to what he had been led to expect, he was charged with possessing the drugs and bailed to appear at court. In conference with the client, a totally different picture emerged from the one presented, both in the prosecution papers and in those from the solicitor. He now claimed that when the Drugs Squad officer came to interview him in the police station he was promised that the charge would be quietly shelved provided that he kept quiet about his role as an informer. Alas, the uniformed arresting officers either did not know about this cosy arrangement, or chose to ignore it, because the offender found himself at a Crown Court, now awaiting trial.

It was only at this late stage that he revealed to me the whole sorry tale including the fact that he had been recruited as an informer and had set up a rather nasty gang of drugs dealers for the Detective. So good was his information and so close was he to the dealers, that he was actually in the house when the police burst in and arrested them. It was so carefully arranged that there was insufficient evidence to charge him, that he could be released without his part in the matter being suspected. If the gang were to get to know of his part in their downfall, he was as he graphically put it, a dead man, but now he was thoroughly compromised, a fact of which he was soon reminded by the drugs officer.

It was not long after his first act as an informer that the Detective was pressing him for further such information. He claimed that he had supplied the Ecstasy tablets with which he was now charged, only to assist the police by marking down a purchaser in the street in the vain hope that they would leave him alone. At first blush, it seemed that this late version of events was unlikely, however he was able to substantiate this story with some very persuasive evidence and it seemed his chances of acquittal were excellent. The only advice that one could properly give to him was to plead not guilty, give evidence on the lines of his instructions and to fight the case with vigour. His fear of being revealed as an informer was so great, however, that he insisted on pleading guilty, forbidding me to offer the court any mitigation which might get back to the people he had been instrumental in putting away. To have fought the case and given evidence would necessarily involve launching an attack on a Senior Detective, effectively accusing him of a serious criminal offence. The possible repercussions were so distressing to contemplate if he were disbelieved, that he would face future peril from both sides. His fears were so real that he was prepared to serve a term of imprisonment rather than take the risks of a trial in open court. He pleaded guilty and was sentenced to a substantial term of imprisonment, but successfully appealed and was soon released.

Although specialist squads figure prominently in instances of corruption, the hand of officers serving or having served in the Flying Squad rests very heavily upon their shoulders by reason of officers being moved from squad to squad. As the first specialist group to be formed, the Flying Squad was regarded as the CID's élite, and their reliance upon informers was summed up in part of a statement read out on The World at One radio programme in 1972, by its head, Commander Kenneth Drury (who was later to appear in the dock at the Central Criminal Court and subsequently imprisoned for serious offences of corruption):

> "The officers of the squad are the finest thief-takers in the world, are dedicated in their work, and carry out their hazardous and sometimes almost impossible duties in the highest tradition of the Metropolitan Police Service.
>
> "To do this it is absolutely essential that they maintain permanent contact with the criminal fraternity, because all their efforts are solely reliant on the work of informants."

This view of the informers' position was a reflection of words written in 1931 by Mr Wensley in his autobiography, *Detective Days*.

> "Pure reasoning is all very well but the blood and bones of all practical Detective work is information. That is to be got in a variety of ways, but the simplest is from informants. I realised that I had to get to know informants and to win their confidence. To that end I laid down one strict rule for myself - always to keep faith. Of course the use of informants - particularly informants who are criminals themselves, has obvious dangers, but anything in the nature of too close an

> intimacy is easily avoided by an intelligent man. Sometimes men or women would seek me out to tell of a projected or accomplished crime. I never asked their motives, although I might guess - revenge, jealousy, spite, the mere desire to curry favour, or it might even be the attempt of a wife or close friend to prevent a man from reverting to evil ways."

The origins of the Flying Squad, a name coined by the press, can be found in the years immediately after the 1914-18 War when many crimes were committed by those who made their escape in cars whilst police pursuers often had to rely upon bicycles. To counter this, the Metropolitan Police formed two groups of officers under the command of a Detective Inspector and expert drivers for each group were sought among serving officers. In addition to skill as drivers, they needed a comprehensive knowledge of London's streets. In 1920, the first groups were formed and given a Crossley tender to carry them. One of the first Flying Squad drivers, George (Jack) Frost, had served as a driver in the Royal Flying Corps until joining the police in 1919 and described the Crossleys as big heavy vehicles with van-type bodies. They had very narrow tyres, no brakes on the front wheels and were difficult to control on wet roads. At least they were faster than bicycles and proved highly effective in that they were able to deliver the squads to the scene of action quickly, whilst there was still a chance of catching them in the act. In due time these groups became a permanent weapon against mobile criminals and raised no objection to the proud title of "Flying Squad" a name donated to them by some headline writer in the daily papers and retained to this day.

The squad developed over the years into an élite group of men and women working at the very sharpest end of the fight against crime. Its officers were, and are, dedicated to catching criminals and in spite of the failures of some members, nothing can detract from the courage, skill and determination of the majority. The success of the Flying Squad was such that a number of other specialist departments were created to deal with different aspects of criminal detection and of these, the intelligence department was one of the most important and effective. In addition, and of importance in events which are now to be discussed, was a department set up to liaise with police outside the Metropolitan area. It hardly needs saying that for such a liaison to be of any value whatsoever, there must be mutual trust between its officers and those Provincial Detectives who turn to them for help. As events proved, the sharing of information in a major inquiry was so tainted as to contaminate relationships between the Met and Detectives working outside London for a long time to come. The inquiry, code named "Operation Coathanger", proved to be the vehicle through which the CID received the biggest shake-up in its history, surpassing even the events of 1877.

Chapter 4

"A Little Firm in a Firm"

On Saturday, November 29, 1969, Gary Lloyd and Julian Mounter, two staff reporters employed by *The Times* newspaper, wrote an article which appeared on the front page under the headlines "Tapes reveal planted evidence" and "London policemen in bribe allegations". The article continued, in part:

> "Disturbing evidence of bribery and corruption among certain London Detectives was handed by *The Times* to Scotland Yard last night.
>
> We have, we believe, proved that at least three Detectives are taking large sums of money in exchange for dropping charges, for being lenient with evidence offered in court, and for allowing a criminal to work unhindered.
>
> Our investigations into the activities of these three men convince us that their cases are not isolated. We cannot prove that other officers are guilty but we believe there is enough suspicion to justify a full inquiry."

Under a subheading "Yard Statement" on the same page:

> "Representatives of *The Times* newspaper called at Scotland Yard at 10 p.m. (last night) and handed in a copy of tomorrow's newspaper together with reels of tape and documents which they said contained signed statements and tape recordings of allegations of bribery and corruption against three London Detectives. The recordings, documents and the newspaper were handed

> to a Senior Detective of 'C1' department of the Criminal Investigation Department at the Yard which deals with serious crime. Notice has been taken of this matter and an inquiry is in hand."

The first leader of that day was headed A LITTLE FIRM IN A FIRM, and these words, alleged to have been said by one of the Detective Sergeants, encapsulated the core of the gathering storm about to break over the CID. Having briefly described the main areas of complaint revealed by the two journalists, the writer went on:

> "Detective Sergeant John Symonds of the Camberwell CID devoted some time to offering advice to the young man (who had complained to the press) on how best to pursue a criminal career. In the course of that advice he implied that he would not be able to help the man if he got into trouble outside London because 'country coppers are swedes' - that is, presumably, that they are too stupid to be corrupt - and elsewhere warnings are given against the uniformed branch in London. There is, however, a claim that this officer was in a position to look after his criminal clients in the Metropolitan area. The key quotation is this: 'I'm in a little firm in a firm anywhere in London I can get on the phone to someone that I know I can trust that talks the same as me' ...
>
> If there is any truth in it, then it suggests that there are at least some other officers who practise the type of methods being employed in this case. *The Times* does not have in its possession evidence which would justify making accusations against other officers, which we

> have to make against the men that we have named, but there are other pieces of evidence which we have handed over which tend to give some support to Sergeant Symonds's boasts."

It was a series of burglaries carried out by a sophisticated group of thieves which set *The Times* on what was then an uncharacteristic crusade. The burglars had prearranged agreements with experienced receivers who had the means to dispose of large quantities of women's high quality clothing so that even before setting out they knew with certainty that whatever they stole had an immediate market. Their technique was a simple one, in that they arrived in the early hours of the morning and having satisfied themselves that there were no police about, parked a van within easy reach, opened up a dress shop with duplicate keys and cleared the entire stock within minutes.

As an example of the technique, one of their crimes was committed within the area where this writer was then serving as a Detective Sergeant. The thieves arrived at about 3 a.m., unlocked a branch of Jaeger's shop whose stock was of a quality affordable only by the wealthier people of the town, and made off leaving nothing but the furniture and fittings. Routine inquiries among people who had been in the area at around that time found a witness who was able to give a description of the thieves' van which was traced to a man living in south London, but of this crime, within the ambit of "Operation Coathanger" as the wider inquiry was named, more later.

So many offences of an identical character were being

reported from all over the country that a squad was set up at Scotland Yard, led by a Metropolitan Detective Inspector and staffed by a mixture of "Met" and county officers. In "Operation Coathanger", the squad had all the necessary ingredients for success. The London officers had their expertise as Detectives, coupled with extensive contacts among the criminal fraternity of the metropolis; the provincial officers brought their own experience and expertise, together with the facility to tap into information from forces throughout the country. Although unstated, it was considered by police outside London that the inclusion of their own men in a squad of this kind gave them a level of control in that they had ears and eyes close to the centre of operations which they could use to try to make certain that there was no trickery. At this period, unhappily, the rank and file Detective serving outside London had more than a little doubt about loyalty and honesty of some metropolitan colleagues. Those doubts and suspicions hardened into certainties all too soon.

The Times allegations of the November 29, 1969 were eventually extended to claim that Detective Inspector Bernard Robson, Detective Sergeant Gordon Harris and Detective Sergeant John Symonds had taken £400 from a young man with a criminal record. The initial purpose of contact between the criminal and the officers was said to have been to engage him as an informer in connection with "Operation Coathanger", but an equally important interest was to extract money from him under threats. The young criminal's identity was not revealed in the article and he was originally referred to by a pseudonym; however, his name, Michael Perry, a man with previous criminal convictions, became public knowledge when court proceedings eventually began. It was he, who having been threatened by the officers, spoke to a friend who put him in touch with a journalist from *The Times*. The newspaper took the inquiry up with enthusiasm and took Perry under their collective wing, preparing him for future meetings with the police suspects.

He was fitted with a concealed microphone and recorder in his clothing with similar equipment installed in his car. His mother's telephone had a listening device attached, and at his meeting with officers there was an undercover photographer at hand to get the best pictures possible. The fact that these inquiries and observations were carried out over a period of about a month without the suspected officers ever being aware of them, says a great deal about the skill and determination of the press people. It also suggests that the nonchalant way in which the officers met and dealt with Perry showed how confident they were that no one would trouble themselves to question what they were doing.

Perry had fallen into the clutches of the "Coathanger" squad as a suspect for the shop burglaries. He claimed that during one of their meetings, Inspector Robson had put into his hand a sausage shaped piece of material, pressing it in and saying "there is the jelly I promised you". Gelignite is commonly packed in cylindrical rolls covered in a grease proof type of paper such as described by Perry, and anyone in the criminal fraternity well knew what "jelly" was. The threat was patently clear to Perry. He understood that if he failed to comply with the officer's demands, his fingerprints on the explosives wrapper, together with perjured evidence could be used to convict him of serious crimes. It was this and other threats that eventually pushed Perry into seeking help, and finding it from the journalists.

At his next meeting with the police officers 11 days later, Perry had been wired up to a pocket tape recorder and transmitter with Lloyd and Mounter in a nearby car listening in. They recorded Robson referring to the gelignite saying "I don't **** play games. When I stuck that in your hand that's there for keeps ... I was going to stitch you ... I told you in the car that with that jelly I would stand there, and believe you me, you could say what you liked and it would make no **** difference. ... You've got off well". The officers were then recorded making demands for money as payment for not having "stitched him up". Much more ominously, they were suggesting that he name a criminal who could be safely charged with receiving stolen goods. It was made clear that the guilt or innocence of the intended victim was irrelevant and they suggested that he might offer the name of someone against whom he had a personal grudge. It may, to the fair minded reader, sound far fetched that an innocent man could be convicted in such a way, but consider the reality of the threats made to Perry and the proposition can be seen in a different light. A few items of property traceable to one of the safe-blowing burglaries being found at his home; a few incriminating answers to questions and the selected victim would have been in real danger of conviction.

All these matters and much more were contained in the papers given to the police by the journalists. However, the response appears to have lacked a spirit of urgency because it was not until February 2, 1971 that proceedings to commit the Detectives for trial were begun. In the interval, Sir Frank Williamson, one of Her Majesty's Inspectors of Constabulary (HMI), had been appointed to oversee the inquiry but after a great deal of hard work he realised that he could expect little co-operation from the CID but instead, a wealth of barely concealed obstruction. Detective Chief Superintendent Lambert, an honest officer untainted by corruption, had been appointed to carry out the inquiry but had been removed from it within a short time without explanation but for reasons which will become obvious later. In his place Detective Chief Superintendent Moody was installed as the investigating officer. HMI Williamson, giving evidence during one of the trials, made it clear that he trusted Lambert but when he had been removed from the inquiry, had great difficulty in accepting Moody in the same way. It seems that Williamson's doubts about Moody were justified because in due time, Moody himself was convicted and sentenced to 12 years' imprisonment at the Central Criminal Court for quite different offences of corruption.

Reporting restrictions were lifted at the request of Mr James Comyn, QC, who appeared for Robson so that, whereas in ordinary circumstances the proceedings would have been in private, the newspapers were able to publish as much of the committal hearing at Wells Street Magistrates' Court as they wished. Whilst the original information from *The Times* gave detail of three officers, Detective Sergeant Symonds was not present at these hearings and the case proceeded against Robson and Harris alone.

The committal hearings lasted for more than two weeks

with defence counsel making spirited attacks on the prosecution witnesses. A main plank of the prosecution case was the recording tapes and the evidence of Mr Perry, whereas the defence claimed that the tapes showed signs of having been interfered with. They were suggesting that the recordings had been subject to interference and, if this were the case, their content had been seriously compromised and could not be relied upon. The magistrate ruled that there was a case to answer and committed both officers to stand trial at the Central Criminal Court on bail. On March 2, 1971, Symonds appeared at Wells Street Magistrates' Court on a variety of charges involving corruption, including obtaining money from Michael Perry as a reward for showing favour. He too was committed to the Central Criminal Court for trial on bail, but breached that bail and went abroad. He did not come to light again until 1980, when he surrendered himself voluntarily at the Central Criminal Court and was taken into custody.

On the day before Robson and Harris were committed for trial and in answer to questions from defence counsel, Detective Chief Superintendent Fred Lambert gave evidence that he had been called back to Scotland Yard to see Mr Colin Webb and Mr Mounter, representatives of *The Times*. "They were making a complaint against certain police officers. I was instructed to investigate this complaint." He added that at about the end of May or in June 1970 he was taken off the investigation "mainly because I disagreed with certain senior officers at Scotland Yard as to how, not this part of the inquiry, but the other part was going to be submitted. I am referring to the allegations made in *The Times*, but not this part of the inquiry. This part was then virtually closed". He did not know why he had been taken off, but "I can surmise, I have since been told that I backed the wrong horse". He went on to say that although he was not ill at the time the inquiry began, he was now on sick leave. He told the magistrate that he had taken a statement from Perry in the course of his inquiries, by means of question and answer. "I do not think that Mr Perry is a man of sufficient intelligence to make a statement of over 100 written pages, to make this type of statement off the cuff". Earlier, whilst giving evidence for the prosecution, Detective Chief Inspector Irving, who had taken a prominent part in the inquiry, gave Robson a glowing character reference in the course of cross-examination by the defence. Solidarity within the CID was adequately demonstrated by this incident in the hearing; nevertheless both Robson and Harris were committed for trial.

In January 1972, more than two years after *The Times'* journalists had published their exposé, the two Detectives were arraigned at the Central Criminal Court before Mr Justice Sebag Shaw. Robson was defended by Mr James Comyn, QC, and Harris by Mr Roger Frisby, QC, both leading counsel of great skill and tenacity. Almost their first task was to seek to have the tape recordings excluded, but after a number of days of protracted legal argument their efforts were in vain when the Judge ruled that evidence to be admissible, a decision upheld by the Court of Appeal. Later in the trial there was much evidence for and against the admissibility of these recordings in a bid to suggest that there had been unlawful interference with the tapes, thus making them unreliable. The jury heard evidence from experts on both sides, in the end preferring the prosecution's view that the tapes were wholly honest and complete.

Detective Sergeant Symonds was out of the jurisdiction and could not be tried with the others. It is often found that when one of a group is missing, it gives the remaining defendants a distinct advantage, because the evidence against the missing defendant is generally inadmissible against the others leaving juries to contemplate substantial holes in the information upon which they must form their opinions. Symonds was said to have been engaged on crimes for his own benefit as well as being part of the Robson/Harris conspiracy, but that damning evidence could not be used in the case of Robson and Harris. However, in spite of this apparent disadvantage, the jury had no difficulty in bringing in guilty verdicts against the officers. Robson was sentenced to eight years' imprisonment and Harris to six.

On March 3, 1981, Symonds appeared at Teesside Crown Court, before His Honour Judge Stroyan, QC, charged with having on three occasions in 1969 corruptly accepted or obtained money as a reward for showing favour to Perry over an arrest. Mr Geoffrey Rivlin, QC, who conducted the case for the Crown, told the jury that it was being held at Middlesborough in the interests of a fair trial outside the "big city" and went on to outline the prosecution allegations:

> "In 1969 Mr Perry was suspected of involvement in a duplicate key burglary at a Co-operative stores in Nuneaton. Four Nuneaton officers went to London and eventually took Mr Perry to Camberwell Police Station,

although there was no hard evidence against him, a fact which Mr Symonds knew.

"Mr Symonds offered the provincial officers his assistance, claiming that he might be able to 'get something out of him' and was allowed to see him in private. In their conversation Mr Symonds, said Mr Rivlin, made no serious attempt to investigate the burglary but was helpful to Mr Perry and gave him advice. The young suspect said that he 'would see him alright'.

"Later, the Nuneaton police who told Mr Symonds that they suspected that an unknown Metropolitan Police Officer had been helpful to Mr Perry, wrote to the young criminal saying no charges would be brought against him.

"Shortly afterwards, in the Detective's car, Mr Symonds asked Perry for a payment of £200."

Sergeant Symonds conducted his own defence and had to be reminded by the Judge on a number of occasions that he was stepping outside the boundaries of what was admissible and what was not. In particular, his cross-examination of prosecution witnesses was far too long and repetitive. He denied all the allegations made against him, claiming that the journalists had acted as *agents provocateurs*, and that Perry had set him up. He told the jury that he had left the country because a message had been passed down to him from the former Detective Superintendent Alfred Moody, that he should do so. It was Moody who conducted the investigations against him 10 years before, but who had himself later been convicted of corruption and imprisoned. One cannot gauge the effectiveness or otherwise of his skills as an advocate, but the jury found him guilty and he was sentenced, still protesting his innocence, to two years' imprisonment.

It was, of course, Symonds's own choice to defend himself, and one does not know how he conducted himself during the trial but it is common experience that untrained people who fall into the trap of trying to ape the language and mannerisms of a professional advocate often manage to make fools of themselves. It is also well understood that the worst lawyers are those who represent themselves. ("The lawyer who acts for himself has a fool for a client".)

Before leaving "Operation Coathanger" I should return to the burglary at a Jaeger shop where valuable information led to the discovery of the suspect vehicle. Information about the crime and particulars of the vehicle used as transport for the stolen goods was passed to a south London police station in whose area the van's owner lived. With exceptional speed and the ability of local officers, we were informed that the van had been traced to a particular street well away from the owner's home and that it was full of brand new clothing. We were assured that two temporary Detective Constables were keeping it under observation with instructions to arrest anyone who came to it. With this heartening news, we left at once and arrived at the police station within the hour with every intention of taking over the observation and making the arrest. However, control of the operation had been passed to officers of the "Coathanger" squad who reported to us that the TDCs had been called away from their observation point to be given updated information and, on their return a few minutes later, had found the van gone. Unhappily they had gone off duty and would not be returning for 24 hours, therefore we could not question them on the reasons for leaving the van. Nor had we the jurisdiction to insist upon seeing them. We parted from our Metropolitan colleagues with open contempt knowing full well that there was nothing we could do to prove what we instinctively knew rather than simply suspected. I must confess to a small smile when the jury returned in the Robson and Davis trial with a resounding verdict of guilty.

Chapter 5

The Advent of Robert Mark

Mr Robert Mark had been Chief Constable of Leicestershire Constabulary for 10 years when in 1967, he was appointed Assistant Commissioner (AC) in the Metropolitan Police under the then Commissioner Sir Joseph Simpson. The higher command structure in the Metropolitan Police was such that immediately below the Commissioner was Deputy Commissioner John Waldron and four Assistant Commissioners, each with responsibility for a specific department within the Service. The deputy had jurisdiction in all four departments at Scotland Yard, but was in command only in the event of the Commissioner himself not being available for some reason. On appointment Robert Mark was put in charge of "D" Department, largely staffed by civilian personnel and which dealt with a whole raft of matters including police dogs, training, welfare, personnel, buildings and many other essential support functions. In his autobiography, he describes the open resentment he experienced within the force about his appointment. Only one outsider had ever been appointed to such high rank in the past and it was made patently clear that the Commissioner, his deputy and the other assistants felt that the job should have gone to a serving member of the Metropolitan force. One day Simpson handed him the copy of a letter from the Home Office which had been circulated to all Chief Officers, inviting applications for appointment to the Chief Constableship of Lancashire. This was one of the country's plum police jobs and when Mark remarked to Simpson that an application for that post, so soon after having been given his new appointment in London, would not be popular at the Home Office, Simpson's unsympathetic retort was to the effect that he had burned his boats.

One of Mark's first priorities was to gain the confidence and co-operation of the other Assistant Commissioners but they, together with Simpson, had been graduates of the Trenchard scheme, a pre-war former Commissioner's attempt to introduce an officer class into the service. It had been considered that, by taking selected young men and introducing them into the service following a year in a collegiate atmosphere, more effective supervisory officers would be produced than by promotion from the ranks. On graduation from the Hendon Police College (not to be confused with the post-war Police College at Bramshill), they were promoted to Station Inspector, a hybrid rank previously unknown, with an expectation of being on a fast track to promotion. It was into this group of graduates from Trenchard's Police College, all close acquaintances over many years, that Mark was installed by the then Home Secretary, James Callaghan.

The chances of breaking down the barriers were few, and if resentment at his appointment was strong amongst many in the force as a whole it was nothing to the anger of the CID, from its Assistant Commissioner (Crime), (AC(Crime)), downwards. It may be that the CID saw the future to be somewhat bleak if Mark, a man with no idea of how their closely guarded internal system worked, were to attain some role in the department's control. No one who had not come up through CID ranks could be expected to appreciate the unique nature of the CID's internal philosophy and practices, nor would they be likely to approve if they knew. The seeds of the Department's future woes were sown when, later, Mark began looking in close detail at discipline within the force and discovered that Detectives were promoted or disciplined by their own senior officers, outside the normal criteria applied to everyone else. Complaints of criminal conduct against a Detective were investigated within the department, once more without reference to any outside authority except the Director of Public Prosecutions to whom a report had to be submitted at the end of the investigation if there was a possibility of prosecution. It was in the DPP's office that a decision to prosecute or not was taken, based upon what the investigator chose to include or omit from his report. In none but the most blatant case was enough evidence available to mount a prosecution against the Detective, and in most such cases no significant disciplinary action followed.

Statistics from an official source showed that even in those relatively few cases where a prosecution was undertaken, 59% of police officers tried on indictment were acquitted, against 17% of the DPP's non-police cases. Juries were understandably reluctant to convict police officers, particularly where evidence of convicted criminals formed a substantial part of the prosecution case. Inquiries into the cases were almost always conducted by officers sympathetic to the accused and protective of the department's reputation so that the enthusiasm of those investigators was not as evident as when dealing with the common criminal. To be fair, a proportion of those acquitted may have been set up by clever thieves for purposes of their own, but it would surely have been rare that an experienced and honest officer could allow himself to be trapped in such a way.

It became clear to Mark that there were dishonest Detectives within the CID with whom the system seemed incapable of dealing and it was against this group that he decided to take up the challenge, much to the eventual discomfiture of the CID and of some of his contemporaries. There were many senior officers totally behind him in his campaign of reform who, when the juggernaut of change had started to roll, were willing to lend a shoulder in order to maintain momentum. These were men who had long resented the scarcely disguised malpractices among CID officers, but had been able do little or nothing about it. The opportunity came when in 1968, following the unexpected death of Sir Joseph Simpson, John Waldron was promoted to Commissioner and Robert Mark to Deputy Commissioner. As Deputy, Mark had no authority over the four Assistants unless the Commissioner was absent. He did, however, have oversight of some areas of their work including discipline although by long standing convention this had excluded the CID.

Allegations of corruption were rolling in, prompted in all probability by the "Coathanger" arrests together with a slowly dawning realisation by the press and others that the CID's invulnerability was at last under a real threat. That threat became reality when an effective complaints department was set up under the designation, A10, of which more later.

Peter Brodie, the AC (Crime) and senior officer responsible for the CID was out of the country attending an international conference, to be followed by an holiday extending his absence to a period of six weeks. In his autobiography, Mark relates the following:

> "From the point of view of C Department he could not have chosen a worse time for so long an absence. During that absence, in the course of a routine conference, the Commissioner unintentionally opened the door through which so many of us wished to walk. Showing signs of despair at the continually increasing number of suspensions he said, 'What can the explanation be? It must be a lack of supervision', which enabled me to reply politely, 'Nothing of the kind. There isn't a person in this room except perhaps the C Department representative, who doesn't know perfectly well that the answer lies in the thoroughly unsatisfactory way in which the CID investigates allegations of crime against its own members. There is ample evidence on the files to prove this beyond doubt ...' The obvious agreement of the others in the room, with the expected exception, clearly shook him, and he said, 'You are the *de facto* disciplinary authority. Why don't you do something about it?' To which I replied, 'Am I to understand that you are giving me the authority to devise, with my colleagues, a means to put an end to all this?' To which he replied 'Yes'."

Mark began to review those cases where officers had been charged with crimes, suspended during inquiries and then been acquitted at their trial. In many of those cases, the officer had been fully restored to duty without any form of disciplinary action being contemplated. Each new case was reviewed with great care and in many instances, clear evidence of serious disciplinary offences were found quite regardless of whatever criminal charge might eventually be laid. In the event of an acquittal the officer would be charged with a disciplinary offence and, if that were proved against him, dealt with in whatever way seemed just. Of course there were protests that officers were being subjected to double jeopardy, but against that proposition there was the effective argument that the charge was of a different nature requiring different proof and having a different ultimate effect. Men in such a situation often decided that it would be better to resign quietly than take the risk of the breach of discipline being proved resulting in their discharge and loss of pension rights.

The new department, A10, was staffed by a combination of uniformed and trustworthy CID officers under the command of the Deputy Commissioner, and was operative for 24 hours a day. All complaints against CID officers, including allegations of crime, were passed at once to the new department and investigated by its own staff to the exclusion, in most instances, of headquarters or divisional CID. The officers of A10 and their supervisors carried out the task with great care and integrity, playing no small part in the formidable labour of cleansing the Detective department. The case load of A10, increased rapidly as it became common knowledge that the bad old days were coming to an end.

On February 27, 1972, the *Sunday People* newspaper published an article alleging that Commander Kenneth

Drury, head of the Flying Squad, had spent two weeks on holiday in Cyprus and Lebanon, with a well-known criminal, James Humphries and his wife "Rusty". The allegation and its possible implications were so serious that an immediate investigation was launched and Robert Mark, by now the Commissioner Designate, suspended the Commander on March 6, to await the outcome of inquiries into possible breaches of the discipline code. It was nine days after Drury's suspension that Mr Peter Brodie AC(Crime) went on sick leave, never to return to duty: Robert Mark was appointed Commissioner on April, 17, 1972, and Drury resigned from the service on May 1, 1972. Drury, as will be seen later, was tried, convicted and sentenced to imprisonment on a matter very closely connected with his erstwhile holiday companion.

The new Commissioner began at once to implement the reforms upon which he had been working for some time. Mr Colin Woods, formerly AC (Traffic) and a formidable officer who was implacably committed to the task of reform, had already been appointed AC(Crime), and plans were afoot to transfer a proportion of Senior Detectives to posts in the uniformed branches, replacing them with senior uniformed men of comparable ranks within the CID. It was also planned to transfer one third of the Flying Squad Detectives each year out of the squad into Divisional police stations so that after three years, there would have been a complete turn round of personnel. Ostensibly it was to broaden the experience of those who were to be transferred whilst at the same time to benefit, by mix of experience, the divisional CID people with whom they would be working. Its more immediate effect was to deal a hammer blow to the cosy relationship between the squad's ranks. Once the "job for life" expectation had been seen to evaporate, it was considered that individual officers would gain in experience and have a wider field of opportunities for promotion. One thing was certain - the self-perpetuating atmosphere of invulnerability was dispersed at a stroke. Of the 478 men who left the force during Mark's time, 402 had either been subject to disciplinary proceedings or had accurately anticipated them. Fifty had been prosecuted and the remainder subjected to proceedings of some kind. Departures under a similar cloud during the preceding 10 years had averaged only 10 per year.

Before looking at the series of trials which exceeded in their seriousness even the "Coathanger" case, a description of a personal brush with suspect CID officers may offer a little light relief, whilst illustrating the networks against which one was often battling.

At the end of 1969, I was engaged in an inquiry into the theft of castings from an aircraft manufacturer's secure store. The castings were of a highly specialised and expensive alloy intended, after considerable machining, to be installed into helicopter engines. Because there is such rigid quality control and stage by stage registration of aircraft components through every process of manufacture, it was possible to say that 30 of these castings had been stolen from the compound over a period of two weeks. An obvious suspect, an engineer employed in the workshop was soon identified, but in spite of every effort, there was never enough evidence to prove the case against him. The value of these items ran into tens of thousands of pounds and although there was little chance of securing a conviction for the theft, it was important to get the castings back if it were possible.

A very discreet source of information pointed to a small local scrap metal merchant as having had them on his premises for a short time before selling them on to one of the big dealers in the Met Police area. As I was obliged to do, I telephoned the provincial liaison office at New Scotland Yard and, without giving precise details of where my inquiry was going to lead, arranged to meet a Detective Inspector from that office at a convenient place nearby. We then drove into the yard of the major dealer and went to the office where we introduced ourselves to an exceptionally well-dressed young man who told us that he was in charge. I outlined the circumstances and described the castings I was looking for, but at no stage suggested that his company had done anything dishonest. He was clearly troubled by our presence, explaining that his father, chairman of the company and the only person with authority to deal with our inquiry, was out to lunch. By now we were in a well-appointed office and he was at great pains to tell us that father's lunch was being taken at the House of Lords, where he was a guest of the late Lord "Bob" Boothby. I explained to him that a few minutes study of the company's purchase record, which all scrap metal dealers were obliged to keep, would probably settle the matter. He left us alone in the office, ostensibly to get his records, but it would seem took the opportunity to make a telephone call to someone at Scotland Yard, because within a short time he returned to ask me to accept a telephone call in the next office. I had told no one outside my own immediate staff of the name and location of the dealers and knew that it could not be them so went, bubbling over with curiosity, to speak to the caller. The conversation went something like this:

> Myself, "Hello".
> Caller, "Superintendent here! ... Fred ?"
> Myself, being economical with the truth ... "Yes".
> Caller ... "Is that c...t from ... shire still there"?
> Myself, "He certainly is, you're talking to him".
> Silence!

The reader must make up his or her own mind about the incident, but to me it revealed a disturbing intimacy between a senior officer and a man who made a living in the world of scrap metal, and worse, his display of utter contempt for a Detective of whom he knew absolutely nothing other than he was outside the magic circle. It would have been interesting to have heard the chairman's view of his son's inability to pick the right Detective when he returned from his tête-à-tête with the noble Lord, a gentleman allegedly on coffee drinking terms with at least one of the infamous Krays and who earlier, whilst an M.P., had been involved in a deal with Czechoslovak gold in 1940, which almost brought his political life to an abrupt end. It would also have been interesting to have overheard the subsequent conversation between the Detective Inspector and his Superintendent who may well have expected some formal complaint to be filed. No complaint was made because one knew that it would have been a waste of time and paper, but worse, could have rebounded through the system upon the low ranking complainant.

***

It is said that "where there's muck there's money", a sample of Yorkshire wisdom well and truly applicable to the scrap metal trade. However, there is a different kind of muck which, without getting one's hands dirty, humping old car engines and the like, makes vast profits for its operators. Without attempting to moralise on the topic, pornography in all its forms with its immense financial investment power can corrupt all kinds of people and in particular law enforcement officers. In the so-called swinging sixties there was a marked change in standards of behaviour and attitude to the almost Victorian *mores* of the time. This is not the place to discuss why this should be, but merely to look at some effects of the change in standards and attitudes, when pornography came to the West End of London with a vengeance. Prostitution in the Soho and surrounding area, together with sex shows, printed and filmed pornography had existed for almost as long as Soho itself, but in the 1950s it became more open with operators of the various activities constantly pushing at the boundaries of legality and what was acceptable. Into this melting pot came elements of the criminal fraternity who quickly established their own areas of control. There is no question of eliminating pornography and its associated activities, however draconian the laws, and their enforcement may be so difficult that the best a police service can ever do is to keep them within reasonable limits. With a vigorous police service determined to prevent the spread of this particular brand of criminal behaviour, the lid could have been put back on the problem. Unhappily, although there was a service in place, the Obscene Publications squad with responsibility for the task, too many of its staff were officers greedy for a share of the profits. Those who preferred to do their job honestly were quickly sidelined and eased out of the squad whenever it was possible for the senior men to arrange it.

On March 1, 1976, after three long years of investigation led by Commander Gilbert Kelland who would later become AC (Crime), 12 Detectives or ex-Detectives who had served at Scotland Yard appeared at Bow Street Magistrates' Court before Mr Barraclough, the Chief Metropolitan Magistrate, charged with conspiracy to receive bribes.

Ex-Commander Wallace Virgo; ex-Detective Chief Superintendent Alfred Moody; ex-Detective Inspector Leslie Alton and ex-Detective Constable Bernard Peter Brown, were charged with conspiring corruptly to receive money and other considerations from persons trading in pornography, between January 1, 1960 and December 31, 1974.

***

Detective Inspector Charles O'Hanlon; Detective Inspector Clive Miles; ex-Detective Chief Inspector Charles Fenwick; ex-Detective Constable Michael Chamberlain and Detective Inspector David Johns were charged with a similarly worded offence, but upon dates between January 1, 1969 and December 31, 1974.

***

Ex-Commander Kenneth Drury, ex-Detective Inspector Alistair Ingram and Detective Inspector John Legge were charged with conspiring corruptly to receive money and other considerations from James William Humphries, between 1970 and 1972.

***

Of the 12 defendants, Mr Drury was a former head of the Flying Squad, whose view on the employment of informers has been set out earlier in the "Coathanger" study. His pronouncement was made on a BBC broadcast when he was asked about a newspaper story in which it was claimed that Detectives from Scotland Yard, incensed by his suspension from duty, had held a meeting in protest. He refuted any suggestion that he had prompted them to hold such a meeting in his support but took the opportunity to give the world his views on their courage and integrity. Instead of quietly sitting it out whilst awaiting the outcome of inquiries, he was once more in the spotlight when, on September 21, 1972, following his retirement, he was called to give evidence in the case of three men charged with conspiring to pervert the court of justice, by attempting to "rig" the acquittal of a group of their associates. In the course of the Crown evidence it was suggested that Drury, together with a number of other Senior Detectives, had been paid sums of money by one of the defendants named Payne. He was called by the defence to give evidence on Payne's behalf and vehemently denied having been offered or taken such bribes. He was followed into the witness box by a number of other ex-senior officers who, it had been alleged, had also taken bribes from Payne although they too denied it. In spite of the heavyweight assembly of defence witnesses who, it seems, failed to convince the jury, Payne and his co-defendants were convicted and imprisoned.

Ex-Commander Virgo had been in charge at various times of the Murder Squad, Obscene Publications Squad and other high profile units. Ex-Detective Inspector Miles was acquitted at the end of his trial and need concern us no further.

James William Humphries, dubbed by the newspapers as "the emperor of pornography " and who was named as one who had paid bribes, was serving eight years' imprisonment for a very serious assault on his wife's alleged lover.

Looking at the list of defendants whilst working on this manuscript it came back to me that I had known some of the 11 Detectives whilst serving as a Detective Sergeant in the mid-sixties. Because relatively small provincial forces were unable to provide specialist instruction courses, the larger forces such as Lancashire, Yorkshire and others provided training for their own officers with places on each course reserved for those from smaller ones. The Metropolitan Police offered the same facility and I therefore found myself nominated to attend a Senior Detective course at Hendon Police Training School, where I found that about half of the students were Metropolitan Sergeants and Inspectors, whilst the other half were provincial officers of similar rank. Apart from we "Swedes" being patronised by some London students and a few instructors, the course was of a very high professional standard, run by teaching staff with many years of active CID work behind them. The course was immensely interesting and important; however, a small dark cloud began to infiltrate the blue sky in the first weeks when we were informed by a senior student that an end of course dinner for the student body was in contemplation. The idea seemed a good one and most people began to look forward to what would undoubtedly be a convivial evening with a last opportunity to cement friendships and contacts from all over the country before returning to our work. Gradually a suggestion was put about that it might be a friendly gesture on our part to invite the instructing staff along as a token of our gratitude for their dedicated efforts on our behalf. There were, of course, mutterings of disapproval about having to fork out for their meals and drinks but, nevertheless, lists of those students who had elected to attend began to circulate. Inevitably there was speculation about what effect a refusal to attend might have, fuelled by the organising students' half-hearted denials that non-attendance could prejudice one's final reports. It was as neat a piece of blackmail as one could imagine but, there we all were in Lyons Corner House on the night, like little lambs to be fleeced for the benefit of highly paid senior officers who could well afford to pay for their own dinners and endless glasses of brandy.

My only memory of the evening was the entertainment. There had been tantalising hints of a spectacular show and in due course, a smooth character in an expensive dinner jacket came on to the stage to introduce the act. He knew a number of the London officers by their first names, including some of the instructors, among whom he seemed to be regarded as a good friend. With lavish praise for a wonderful act, he introduced - a stripper. She gyrated among the audience shedding her quick release outfit piece by piece until one foolish, middle-aged Sergeant, from Birmingham stroked her bottom as she waltzed away from him. Quick as lightening she turned and slapped his face with the all the force she could muster, leaving a very red faced gentleman rocking on his chair and a delighted audience rocking on theirs. The show eventually ended with the presenter draping a gown around the now fully naked girl, who left to ecstatic applause.

This little episode, recalled after so many years, has a bearing on what is to come. First, the degree of intimacy between a sleazy showman and Senior Detectives was clearly undesirable and, secondly, the show itself would have attracted prosecution had it been given in a public theatre; finally, one of the students and one of my instructors figured as defendants in the porn trials to come.

Chapter 6

Obscene Publications Squad - The First Prosecution

For the previous 20 years there had been a group of men making their living from pornography in London's West End. Very little film or video pornographic material was actually produced in the UK in the early days, and sources of supply included Holland, the USA and Denmark, where there seemed to be few problems in filming and printing the most graphic examples. The law in the UK is now contained in the Obscene Publications Acts of 1959 and 1964, in which it is laid down that one who publishes an obscene article, whether for gain or not or has an obscene article for gain, commits an offence punishable by six months' imprisonment summarily, or three years on indictment. In the Act "article" means any description of article containing or embodying matter to be read or looked at or both, any sound record, and any film or other record of a picture or pictures. In the broadest of terms, an obscene article is something which tends to deprave and corrupt. This is not the forum to define obscenity any further - there is a large body of case-law devoted to the subject and perhaps a sufficient test for this purpose is to say that, for the most part, one recognises it when one sees it. Obscenity, as displayed in the merchandise of Soho's porn bosses, is instantly recognisable.

There has always been a loosely connected group of men at the forefront of criminal activities in the West End of London, and with increasing availability of pornographic films, video recordings and magazines, part of the group began to concentrate their efforts on cultivating this promising sex market and maximising their profits from it.

Supposedly on the opposite side in a battle to control the worst excesses of the industry was C1 Branch, staffed by CID officers, which became the unfortunate bearer of a string of names of which the "Dirty Squad" was just one. Its official title was the Obscene Publications Squad and if ever an investigative body needed integrity and total honesty in its members, this was surely among the first. It is impossible to pinpoint a time when porn bosses and corrupt officers came together but in the 50s and 60s a virtual partnership between some of them had been established. From then on, any officer transferred into the Squad was quickly integrated into the existing culture, learned to live with its practices, or moved back into general detective duties.

It may already have occurred to some readers to ask why it was necessary to employ highly trained CID officers to be responsible for obscene publications and associated matters. Officers seconded from the uniformed branch and operating in plain clothes for a limited period could have made a sufficient contribution as they had done in street betting matters for many years. Of course there would be a need from time-to-time for specialist help in sophisticated methods of detection, but the basis of the trade, and hence its control, should be relatively simple. Buy the material on the continent or USA; arrange for safe passage into the country; distribute the product into existing outlets; and collect the profit on sales! Whenever something more than intelligent observation and inquiries was needed, CID officers working in harmony with the uniformed branch could have played their specialised role without engaging in the old practices. There was no legitimate place for a closed-shop group of Detectives in Soho, particularly when that shop was riddled with corruption. In the end, the CID lost its monopoly of the task which was undertaken by a mixed team of officers, but only after a long investigation leading to three major criminal trials.

Amongst the most influential of the porn barons were Bernie Silver, Frank Mifsud, John Mason and James Humphries. Not always in total harmony, they and a few others carved up the pornographic trade as an extra to the running of brothels and street prostitutes. None of them were strangers to violence in the settlement of disputes nor in the protection of their individual turf. Soho had, at its peak period, no fewer than 40 shops under criminal control selling books, magazines, film and video recordings. There was no statutory licensing system to regulate the content of the material sold by them and the only sanction was criminal prosecution.

A system of licensing did exist, however, but it was unofficial and whether or not a trader could benefit by subscribing to it depended upon his position in the hierarchy. The licensors were members of the Obscene Publications Squad and the right to keep a dirty bookshop rested with them. In the course of the trials, a number of the porn shop operators gave evidence against one or more of the Detectives, and it emerged that in order to open a new shop within the area they would be obliged to contribute a large "licence" fee, followed by a periodic top-up. Failure to pay the weekly or monthly top-up would result in the backslider's outlet being targeted by members of the squad for special attention, such as questioning every customer on their leaving the shop and demanding to see what they had bought, often to their great embarrassment, and searching the premises several times a month. Enforcement of the rules was seldom necessary: nor was it easy to get a licence, because neither the squad nor the pornographers welcomed the dilution of profits by allowing an increase in outlets.

No Specialist Squad could continue to operate without being able to demonstrate some degree of success, so a steady procession of porn dealers passed through the magistrates' courts charged with offences under the Act, to which a guilty plea was almost always entered. The appearance of any dealer of substance was rare; more often than not the face in the dock was that of a manager prepared to bear the punishment due to the true operator. All fines imposed by the courts were assimilated as part of the business expenses and, although they could not be charged as a taxable expense, a very limited amount of tax was computed as payable in any event. Occasionally things went a little wrong and the boss's surrogate found himself, to his surprise, en route to one of Her Majesty's prisons instead of going to the court clerk's office with cheque book in hand.

The first of the porn trials began at the Central Criminal Court on November 8, 1976, before Mr Justice Mars-Jones; to have joined all 11 defendants in one indictment would have resulted in an unmanageable trial, impossible for even the most intelligent of juries to be able to comprehend. In the dock were retired Chief-Inspector George Fenwick, Detective Inspector Clive Miles, Detective Constable Michael Chamberlain, Detective Inspector David Johns, Detective Sergeant Peter Fisher and Detective Inspector Charles O'Hanlon. All were charged together with conspiring corruptly to receive money or gifts between 1964 and 1973. There were in addition, 20 substantive charges of accepting bribes levelled against individual defendants to which they all pleaded not guilty. The prosecution case was opened by Mr John Mathew, who said:

> "This is a story that can only be described as a cancerous growth of corruption which spread itself through the Obscene Publications Squad, commonly known as the 'Porn Squad', at Scotland Yard from the most junior to the most senior officers over many years. The main period involved in this trial is between 1970 and 1972, although the allegation is that the Pornographic Squad had engaged in an almost unbelievable practice of bribery which began in the 1950s, had gone on into the 1960s, and finally into the 1970s.
>
> Proprietors of pornographic shops in the West End had paid thousands of pounds for the licence to trade. No pornographic shop could open without a down payment of £1,000, and then further regular payments had to be made or else it would be raided and its stock seized.
>
> If the proprietor paid his initial licence fee and then monthly payments afterwards he was allowed to trade unhindered or was even helped if the premises had to be raided because of complaints. If a shop had to be raided the owner would be warned so that he could dispose of his stock of hard porn in time, and if prosecution had to follow, he might be allowed to substitute some other person with no previous convictions to face proceedings."

Mr Mathew told the jury that during the material time, Chief-Inspector Fenwick was in day-to-day charge of the Squad and had under him an Inspector and a number of Sergeants and Constables. The convention grew up that on Friday nights, the Squad would be entertained by some of the porn operators and the junior officers would receive a share of the week's takings from their seniors. He continued: "Some of those junior officers found themselves caught up in a web from the moment they joined the squad and were then either corrupted by other senior officers or found themselves compromised with no one to turn to because everyone was involved from the Commander downwards". He went on: "The swinging sixties, with their liberated thought and the advent of a more permissive society, brought as a side wind an enormous growth in the sales of pornography. Shops blossomed in the West End, but only those that paid money to the Pornography Squad actually thrived and flourished. The profits were enormous. In one Rupert Street shop in the late 1960s the two proprietors each took £1,500 cash weekly from the business. They could easily afford to pay for the licence to trade". He told the jury that although there had been a press exposé in 1970 and inquiries made, it was in 1973 that the then Assistant Commissioner, Gilbert Kelland, was put in charge of matters when diaries from one of the porn merchants came into his possession.

Before calling the Crown evidence, Mr Mathew gave the jury a clear warning that he would be calling a number of witnesses who were themselves involved in the porn trade. "Virtually all of them have convictions and are of a dubious character, so their testimony would have to be regarded with care".

This vitally important warning was repeated to the jury on many occasions throughout the trial by counsel for the defendants and by the judge in his summing up. Regardless of the nature of a charge against an officer, where a witness with previous convictions stands to be measured against him, the odds are weighted in favour of the policeman as indeed they should be. It is only when a jury having heard all the evidence is satisfied that the officer is indeed guilty that those odds have changed.

Gilbert Kelland together with a small but dedicated band of officers had been investigating the porn allegations for some time before achieving a major breakthrough. They knew perfectly well who the suspected Detectives were and had no doubt as to the identity of the porn operators who had been paying them off. By painstaking efforts the team were able to discover from sources such as restaurant booking records and the like, the many occasions when lavish entertainment and other gifts and favours had been provided for members of the squad by either Silver or Humphries. Travel records, officers' leave dates and many other sources of information were meticulously tracked down and indexed. Suspects and witnesses were identified, photographed and their personal details logged into the system until there was little concealed from the investigators. The crowning material came in the contents of Humphries' diaries obtained from his wife whilst he was in prison, eventually to be followed by his agreement to give evidence against the Detectives. He had firmly declined to co-operate with Mr Kelland for a long time, refusing to admit to any contact with porn squad officers. However, he had a change of heart, partly as a result of Mr Kelland's patient handling of him and partly because of his disillusion with Drury whom, he claimed, had put the story about that Humphries was "a grass"- a police informer. Nothing could be more damaging to a man living in Humphries's environment where to be labelled an informer creates a host of deadly enemies. When he did open up to the investigating team, it was to reveal the whole extent of the Squad's corruption.

The first Crown witness was Ronald Mason, a self-confessed trader in pornography, who had served a 12-month sentence and paid £25,000 in fines for offences against the Obscene Publications Act, during more than 20 years in the business. He told the jury that he had been paying bribes to police officers during the whole of that time, beginning in about 1950 and continuing until the whole matter came to light. In the early days, the payment was in the order of £300 a month, but by about 1970, it had escalated to £1,000 a month. The regular practice was for him to meet a Detective Inspector for lunch at the White House Hotel, Albany, where he would leave the money between the pages of a newspaper either on the bar or a seat from where his guest would pick it up. At the time he was living in Barcelona and made a round trip on pre-arranged dates to pay his dues. The departure of an officer on promotion was not allowed to interfere with the smooth flow of money from him to the Squad for on an occasion when a senior officer of the Squad left on promotion, Mason was, as he put it ... "handed over to Fenwick".

An easy intimacy existed between them and whenever he was at his Surrey home on Sundays during 1970 and 1971, he would entertain some members of the Porn Squad to lunch time drinks. He recalled that Fenwick and Johns had visited on at least 10 of those occasions, and O'Hanlon once. In the course of cross-examination for one of the defendants, Mason denied that he was corrupting the police officers to whom he gave money, if indeed he had done so but his answer to that was, "I was not corrupting anyone - I was being blackmailed". Mason went on to explain that he paid £1,000 each month for the sole purpose of being allowed to keep his shops open. He knew that if he did not pay, it would be quite easy for every customer leaving the shop to be searched, and on occasions his shops were searched.

Mr Mathew: "Did you know about them in advance?"
Mr Mason: "Yes. Invariably a telephone call would be made to the leaseholder of one of my shops and the codeword 'W.H. Smiths' would be mentioned. In great haste much of the hard porn would be moved and often just one box of porn would be left for the police to seize".

Thirteen porn merchants were called for the Crown during the prosecution case and their evidence, taken as a whole, involved each of the defendants in some significant ways. Among their assertions was that it was commonplace to be tipped off when a raid was to take place and that it would not be sensible to clean out every item of pornographic material. So it was that when the search warrant was executed, some material would be found and confiscated resulting in either a relatively minor charge against a front man with no convictions, or the material would be sold back to the dealer at half its market value. Some of the particular allegations made by witnesses were that one, a Mr Wallace, had paid £9,500 to Fenwick, whilst another, Terrence Nicholl, had been paying £40 each week over a period of two years in return for being warned of impending raids.

The blanket defence of all defendants was that they had never asked for or received money from any of the witnesses. That there was some unusual money circulating within the Squad is beyond doubt, because the most damaging Crown witness was Detective Inspector Anthony Kilkeer who had held the rank of Detective Sergeant in the Squad in 1971. He had only been with them for two weeks when, at the Friday night drinks session, he was given some bank notes by Fenwick. His protests that he did not want money were overridden by Fenwick stuffing the notes into his jacket pocket, a situation that left him confused and embarrassed. The only explanation Fenwick offered for giving him the money was that it was a share out, backing up his words by telling the officer that it was the easiest money he would ever get. It was safe money. He had nothing to worry about. When Kilkeer left the office he threw the money away in the street. However, each Friday evening from then on he was given further amounts in an envelope containing between £10 and £20, by one or other of his seniors, all of which he allowed to accumulate in his desk drawer. Understandably, this junior officer felt trapped. He had been deliberately introduced into a corrupt system by the very man with responsibility for ensuring that the Squad was run honestly. He felt that he had no alternative but to go along with whatever was going on until an opportunity arose to seek transfer to a different CID department.

At one stage, Inspector O'Hanlon saw the envelopes in his desk and pointed out that the bank notes in them could be easily seen and he asked what they were. Kilkeer told him "You know. You have been giving it to me each week". He described events at the Squad's Annual Christmas party at a London restaurant. Things began to get out of hand because there was too much drinking. "It was all going; it seemed that money was no object", he said, "The whole thing welled up in me, thinking about loyalty to the service, and it seemed to me that I was an arch hypocrite". He said that he felt disgusted and wanted to leave the party and went towards the cloakroom. He then realised that he was being followed by three of the defendants who told him "you are involved". It seems that he was suspected by other members of the Squad as being less than wholehearted about the system because one of them, Mr Fisher, accused him of being a spy planted in the Squad and went on to say, "Don't worry. If we all get nicked we can always form a football team on the Isle of Wight", no doubt a reference to HM Prison Parkhurst.

It was during the course of a three-day torment of Kilkeer in the witness box that the defence showed their hand when, being cross-examined by Mr Edward Gardner, QC, it was suggested that money distributed to Squad members had been collected from people who had been allowed to borrow pornographic films from the Squad's stores to show to paying audiences. Police officers from outside the Squad had been allowed to see pornographic material on occasions, but Kilkeer told Mr Justice Mars-Jones and the jury that no one should run away with the idea that the Squad's office was some kind of cinema club where people could see a "blue" film if they wished. Nor could he recall Manchester United football team being one of the audiences as suggested by Mr Gardner. Nothing further was heard of this particular suggestion which, had it been possible to prove, would have delighted the press.

In the course of his evidence, in answer to questions why he had not reported corruption within the Squad, he explained that he had been warned by colleagues of what could happen to him if he did. Nobody would believe him and he would face the chance of being thrown out of the force as medically unfit. It was the system at Scotland Yard and he had to stick to it. It was impossible to do anything about it and the senior officers did not want to admit that corruption existed. Mr Kilkeer's courage in giving evidence against his former colleagues was immense and his example encouraged other officers who had been subjected to entrapment into the corrupt system to come forward. The prosecution evidence became increasingly hard to counter and one gets the feeling, in making a short review of the trial some 20 years or more later, that it was the point at which the defence of all but one of the accused officers crumbled away.

The novel story put forward by Mr Gardner, QC, on his client's instructions was elaborated upon when Mr O'Hanlon gave evidence in his own defence. The essence of what he had to say was that whilst there had been distributions of insignificant amounts of money, this had come from other police officers who had paid to borrow films for showing at stag parties and the like. He claimed to have paid only two sums of money to Mr Kilkeer and similar amounts to Sergeant Ian Monroe who had also given evidence for the Crown. These sums totalled £50 between the two officers and, "that was money given to me by other police officers for lending them obscene films". He also admitted having given five officers £10 each, keeping £10 for himself just before Christmas 1971. He refused to give the names of those officers who had paid him for the rental of films in spite of being ordered to do so by the Judge. He said, "The money came from police officers. I cannot name them. They are serving police officers and they are absolutely terrified."

At the end of a trial lasting some six weeks, all but ex-Detective Inspector Miles were convicted and sentenced to terms of imprisonment ranging from 10 years for Fenwick; eight years for Chamberlain; seven years each for Johns and O'Hanlon; and four years for Fisher. At various stages towards the end of the trial Mr Justice Mars-Jones persisted in his questions as to where all the money had gone but with no satisfactory answers. This should not have come as a great surprise to him in view of their blanket denial of having been given any significant amounts. After conviction, when the jury were entitled to know more about the defendants, it was revealed that two of them bought two hire car companies, whilst others had formed a development company, although it had not apparently traded. This information may have gone some way to satisfy the trial judge's curiosity, but it did not give him the opportunity to impose some kind of monetary penalty in addition to the sentences of imprisonment.

At the conclusion of this, the first of three linked trials, those who had worked so hard to investigate and present the prosecution case had every reason to feel satisfied. But it was not yet all over, for there were two more groups of disgraced officers still awaiting trial.

Chapter 7

Defective Paperwork by Design

The second trial in the series began at the Central Criminal Court on February 28, 1977, before Mr Justice Mars-Jones. In the dock were ex-Commander Wallace Virgo; ex-Detective Chief Superintendent Alfred Moody; ex-Detective Inspector Rodney Tilley; ex-Inspector Leslie Alton; ex-Detective Constable Peter Brown and Detective Sergeant Gordon Hamer, a man who was still a serving officer but presently suspended. They were charged with a total of 27 counts of conspiracy and corruption to which they all pleaded not guilty. David Tudor Price, QC, opened the case for the Crown.

Mr Price told the jury during his opening speech that Commander Virgo was paid £2,000 a month in bribe money. He said that in January 1970, Bernard Silver, a well-known Soho criminal, and James Humphries, a Soho strip club and property owner, met Mr Virgo at the Ile de France restaurant in Jermyn Street, Piccadilly. There, according to Mr Humphries, Mr Virgo said he was upset because he was receiving only £1,000 out of the £10,000 that Mr Humphries had said was being paid to Detective Chief Superintendent Alfred Moody, the officer in charge of the Obscene Publications Squad, for a "licence" to run obscene bookshops in the West End.

Mr Humphries told Mr Virgo to ask Moody for more money, counsel said, but Mr Virgo replied that he had done so but all Moody would say was that the money had "gone upstairs." What is meant by "upstairs" is a matter of inference. But in Scotland Yard, the evidence will be, that it is on the top floor where most of the senior officers are accommodated. The inference is that he had paid the money to somebody more senior than Virgo. [There were only three ranks above a Commander, namely a Deputy Assistant Commissioner, Assistant Commissioner and the Commissioner himself.] He said an arrangement was then made that Mr Virgo should receive £500 a week, payable at the rate of £2,000 a month, with an extra payment of £2,000 at Christmas.

Having given the jury a broad outline of the facts that it was intended to prove, the prosecutor went on to explain the elements of law involved in the charges; reminded them of the burden and standard of proof required, and cautioned them to treat the witnesses who had been shown to be of bad character with great care. With that he called the first of the Crown witnesses, James Humphries.

Humphries told the court that he knew Mr Moody, Mr Virgo, Mr Tilley and Mr Brown, and had seen the other two defendants. In 1969, when he told Mr Virgo he could not get "licences" for his bookshops, Mr Virgo told him: "I can soon arrange that. Bill Moody was my old Squad Sergeant and I'll speak to him". Mr Humphries said he would give him £1,000. They went into the lavatory together where he gave Mr Virgo £50. Some days later Mr Humphries went with Mr Silver to the Empress restaurant, in Berkeley Street, where he met Mr Moody.

A conversation followed about a "licence" for 55 Rupert Street. Mr Humphries said that at a second meeting they agreed on a £4,000 down payment and £100 a week.

"I had £2,000 in a brown paper bag and Silver had a brown paper bag as well. I gave my bag to Silver and in my presence he handed the two bags to Bill Moody". He went on to say that after he had opened the shop, he met Mr Virgo in Doll's Club in Shepherd Market and gave him the £1,000 he had been promised.

Humphries was cross-examined at great length by various defence counsel but maintained the essentials of his evidence. He admitted that he was currently serving a sentence of eight years' imprisonment for his part in a knife attack on his wife's lover, but stoutly maintained that he was innocent of that crime. His financial situation was examined in great detail and he told the jury that, apart from his pornographic bookshops, which earned him close on a quarter of a million pounds over three years, his interests extended to international pornography, sex boutiques and strip clubs. When he was asked if his income from all these sources was nearer £500,000, he replied that he did not keep books of account but estimated that his income was in the order of £100,000 a year in cash. He agreed that he had owned a villa in Ibiza, a yacht and a farm in England, and that he had bought his wife two Rolls Royces and a Mercedes at various times. By the end of his days in the witness box, it had become clear to the jury that talk about large sums of money floating about among squad members had a solid basis in possibility, if not in fact. That he dispensed large sums could hardly be doubted, and neither could his claim that over the years he had paid sums of money to 42 police officers, all of whom were recorded in his diary.

A mini-cab driver by the name of Sirkin was called as a witness for the Crown and he related the story of how, in 1967, he came to serve six months' imprisonment for selling obscene material. He had pleaded guilty to the charge in spite of not having been on the premises at the material time, nor having anything whatever to do with the material, but had masqueraded as the defendant before the magistrate, in place of a friend, William Hicks, who was the real offender. Hicks, who would almost certainly have been imprisoned as a result of having previous convictions for the same offence, asked him to take his place in court and accept the sentence in his own name. The switch was carried out with the full knowledge and consent of the Detective in charge of the case, who assured him that he would merely be fined and that Hicks would pay it. Sirkin no doubt weighed up the disadvantage of acquiring a relatively minor conviction against a payment of £500, and went for the cash option. To the apparent surprise of the Detective, and the horror of Sirkin, the magistrate decided that a six months' jail sentence was more appropriate than a fine. Sirkin entered a notice of appeal against the sentence and was granted bail to await the hearing. He told the jury that the same Detective advised him not to appear at the appeal because it would not be allowed and he would go immediately into custody to serve the term imposed on him. The police would take care not to find him, however, so that, in effect, he was in the clear. A year later Sirkin, stricken by conscience, surrendered himself to the court and went straight to prison. One cannot be sure quite what was in the magistrate's mind in sentencing Sirkin in a way that was outside the normal range, but perhaps he suspected something and was tempting the authors of the scheme to try again before a judge on appeal and was offering them more rope.

Mr Frederick Lambert, formerly a Detective Chief Superintendent was also called as a Crown witness. He gave evidence of a period when he was responsible for supervising some of the Porn Squad officers' case reports. He had read paperwork prepared for submission to the Director of Public Prosecutions and, finding it inadequate, sent it back to the officers responsible with instructions that they make further inquiry and provide proper details. It has been suggested earlier in this book that where there were hidden interests at work, defective case files were sometimes sent to the DPP in the full knowledge that they contained insufficient evidence for a prosecution to have a reasonable chance of success or were irretrievably defective in some other way.

The mechanics involved in preparing prosecution files for any crime were that a case was allocated to a particular officer, usually the arresting officer, who had the responsibility to assemble all available evidence and prepare a covering report. These papers would be submitted to the supervisory officer whose job was to check that all had been done that should have been done. He would look at the proposed charge or charges, and satisfy himself that there was admissible evidence to support them in the papers. If everything was satisfactory he would endorse the report with a recommendation to prosecute, but if there were any holes in the case he would send the papers back to the originating officer for further inquiries. On the rare occasions when the defect could not be cured he would be bound to recommend that there should be no prosecution. The next supervisory officer would carry out a similar exercise and, unless he were able to spot some flaw, forward the papers with his recommendation. By the time the case papers reached their final stage at which a decision must be made any loose ends should have been neatly tied up for an informed judgment to be made. This, of course, presumes that supervisors have taken an objective view of the case. Otherwise, the whole exercise is merely cosmetic and intended to cover up corruption.

It was when Mr Lambert found that reports he was supposed to forward to the DPP were inadequate or required clarification in areas which seemed doubtful, his responsibilities were changed. For the second time he found himself removed from a position where there was a danger of his discovering anomalies and interfering with the *status quo*. The first occasion was in the "Coathanger" inquiry when he had been removed and replaced by none other than Chief Superintendent Moody. And now he had fallen foul of Wallace Virgo, then head of the Obscene Publications Squad, who accused him of upsetting the department by unnecessarily rejecting case reports submitted by Squad Detectives. Mr Lambert had clearly had enough and retired from the police on medical grounds in March 1971. If a man of Lambert's rank and experience could be so neutralised, what chance was there that disenchanted officers of more lowly rank could make effective protest?

He was vigorously cross-examined by Mr Donald Farquharson, QC, for the defence of Wallace Virgo but, in spite of an unpleasant and irrelevant attack on his personal life by raking over an affair he had once had, the defence gained nothing from him. Among other things it was suggested to him that his ineffectiveness as a Detective officer was the reason he had been removed from the "Coathanger" inquiry. In fact, the vehemence of the personal attack upon him and this wholly incorrect assertion prompted the prosecution to call evidence in rebuttal. They called Frank Williamson, the former HMI who had been inquiring into "Coathanger". He expressed his complete satisfaction with Lambert's work when under his command, but quite the opposite with Moody's past efforts.

Mr Moody gave evidence in his own defence and told the jury that the first time he saw John Mason was at Scotland Yard where he was being interviewed by other officers in 1965. There had been a bombing incident in one of Mason's Soho shops and it was believed that a protection racket was being set up in the West End. He claimed not to know that Mason was a trader in pornography and denied that he had ever been paid by Mason for any purpose. He agreed in cross-examination that although, on the evidence he had heard, there was corruption in the Obscene Publications Squad on a considerable scale, he did not know of it at the time, although he had served on the Squad for a total period of three years. Allegations made by his former colleagues who had given evidence and claimed that he had organized collection and distribution of the corrupt funds were "all malicious allegations" and wholly untrue. His testimony failed to shake the prosecution case and the evidence linking him to Humphries and Mason, through those gentlemen and from the mouths of his former colleagues, provided the jury with sufficient reason to find him guilty.

Mr Virgo, too, gave evidence and denied having

received money from either Humphries, Silver or Mason whom he had first met during inquiries into the death of Freddie Mills, the well-known boxer. His counsel asked, "Humphries claims that on half a dozen occasions in 1970 he paid you himself sums of £2,000 and on other occasions so did Silver?" Virgo replied, "That is completely untrue". He told the court that he was so concerned to avoid corruption within the Squad that he would stress to its members at monthly intervals the need for vigilance.

Of the remaining defendants, ex-Detective Inspector Tilley pleaded guilty to one of the three charges against him and gave evidence for the Crown. That evidence was utterly devastating and it was therefore essential for his credibility to be destroyed by other defence counsel if at all possible. In cross-examination on behalf of ex-Inspector Alton, he freely admitted that his object in giving Queen's evidence was to tell the truth for his own sake in the hope that the Judge would minimise the sentence to be passed on him. It was against this background that he told the court what happened at the Friday night share-outs. He described a procession of officers going into the Squad's property store and emerging with their money, after which all members of the squad were expected to attend a drinks party at a local pub. It was Mr Alton who made it his business to see that most members attended and there was a lot of heavy drinking, he himself spending about £10 on each occasion, a considerable amount when compared with an officer's salary at that time.

It was only 10 days after joining the Squad that the first moves to corrupt him were made when Detective Sergeant

Andrews took him to lunch near Scotland Yard and handed him a brown envelope containing £10 saying, "That is for doing as you are told and keeping your mouth shut". He went on to say that he received similar corrupt payments almost weekly. He recounted another incident when, returning to Scotland Yard in a taxi, another Detective Sergeant had pulled out some bank notes and began putting them into envelopes, remarking as he did so, "I'd better make up the wages". He was handed one of the envelopes.

Leslie Alton, a former Detective Inspector gave evidence in his own defence and told the jury that he was never knowingly a party to the distribution of bribes to Squad members, nor that he had ever received money from pornography dealers. The suggestion that he had sold pornographic materials back to porn dealers was "a wicked lie". He also denied with some vehemence that he had ever received money from pornographers let alone the enormous sum of over £6,000. As a Detective Constable in the West End from 1955 until 1958, he was aware that bookshops were flourishing around Soho as they had when he visited the district as a young soldier some years earlier. "From that time I had formed the view that it was political to allow them to flourish. I remember being in Soho as a young Detective Constable and it was not uncommon to see celebrities and politicians using the bookshops". When he was posted to the Obscene Publications Squad in July 1966, he had adopted the policies dictated by his senior officers at Scotland Yard. He was told to carry out his duties with extreme caution when dealing with obscene publications. Everything was be done through the Director of Public Prosecutions and he was told that the Squad was "under the political spotlight" in relation to censorship and human rights. "I was told that insofar as shops in Soho were concerned, to be cautious and not try to wipe them out, but to harass them to the best of my ability".

Bernard Brown, a former Detective Constable gave his evidence next and, apart from a blanket denial of all the points put to him by the prosecution, had little to add to take the case forward to any great degree. He was followed by Sergeant David Hamer, still a serving officer. He too denied the allegations against him in detail. He said, "I have never been offered money of any kind corruptly by any police officer during my police service and I have never accepted money of any kind from any pornographer". He went on to say that he had never seen the distribution of envelopes containing money to members of the Squad. With his evidence completed, there remained only speeches by all counsel and the judge's summing-up.

So long and detailed had been the evidence in the trial that Mr Justice Mars-Jones took almost four days to sum up the case. When the jury were instructed to retire to consider their verdicts it was obvious that they would need a considerable time. They were in retirement for several days and, as was the law until recently, could not separate until reaching their final verdicts, being obliged to spend three nights in a hotel. During the course of their deliberations, they came back into court on a number of occasions to announce such verdicts as they had reached, convicting on some counts against some defendants and acquitting on others but, at the end of their efforts, they returned verdicts of guilty of conspiracy to accept bribes against each of the six defendants.

Alfred Moody, the former Detective Chief Superintendent who had been described as "the main architect of this conspiracy of corruption", was sentenced to 12 years' imprisonment and ordered to pay £10,000 towards his legal costs.

Wallace Virgo, formerly a commander who was at one time in charge of Scotland Yard's 3,500 Detectives, was sent to prison for 12 years and ordered to pay £15,000 towards his legal costs. In his case a successful appeal against that conviction resulted in his release from prison during the following year.

Leslie Alton, formerly a Detective Inspector and described by the Judge as being "almost in the same class as Moody" was sent to prison for 10 years and ordered to pay £5,000 costs.

Bernard Brown, formerly a Detective Constable, was sent to prison for seven years.

David Hamer, formerly a suspended Detective Sergeant, was sent to prison for four years.

Rodney Tilley, formerly a Detective Constable was sent to prison for three years.

After the prisoners had been taken down to the cells, the Judge paid a glowing tribute to Sir Robert Mark and his men, and to the press for their valuable part in bringing the matter into the light. He commended the senior officers in charge of the investigation. They had discharged their duties impartially, "... and the cancer of corruption which existed in the Obscene Publications Squad has been exposed and exorcised".

But there was yet one final trial in the series to come.

Chapter 8

Difficulties of Presenting Evidence

On June 14, at the Central Criminal Court, the trial began of former Commander Kenneth Drury, John Legge a Detective Inspector under suspension, and former Detective Inspector Alistair Ingram. The indictment against them alleged a total of 14 counts of receiving bribes from James Humphries, although each faced a different specific charge within that total. They all pleaded not guilty. Mr Justice Peter Payne presided over the trial: Mr Davis Tudor Price conducted the prosecution, Mr George Schindler represented Drury and the two remaining defendants had counsel acting on their behalf.

This case differed from the other two in the series in that the defendants had not been involved in the activities, legitimate or otherwise, of the Obscene Publications Squad but the link was forged through the presence of James Humphries, a witness for the Crown and his association with Drury, Ingram and most of the officers convicted in those earlier trials. In opening the Crown's case Mr Tudor Price described Humphries as a former prominent criminal in Soho, concerned with pornography, prostitution and strip clubs. He said of the defendants that "they were indebting themselves to this tycoon who was putting himself outside the law".

Mr Tudor Price said that during 1971 and 1972, Mr Drury was on Mr Humphries' payroll, receiving about £5000 in cash and a similar sum in kind, "so that he could have a friend in the police who could assist him in time of trouble". In February 1972 the *Sunday People* published an article alleging that Commander Drury and his wife had spent a holiday in Cyprus with Humphries and his wife "Rusty" with the clear implication that there was a basis of corruption in the visit. When questioned about the visit, Drury gave an explanation to the effect that Humphries was a good informant with information that Ronald Biggs, one of the "Great Train Robbery" defendants and an escapee from prison, was hiding on the island. Unwisely, Drury had not passed this information on to his superiors, nor informed them of his visit to Cyprus and its supposed purpose. Dealing with the case against Ingram, Mr Tudor Price put him as a much lesser figure who supplied Humphries with inside information for reward. Mr Legge, he said, owed his position in the dock in large measure to Mr Drury telling the court that he had benefited by receiving bribes from Mr Humphries to please Mr Drury.

In opening a case to a jury, prosecuting counsel has the duty to outline the case he proposes to put before them in a restrained and clear review taken from the evidence he has in his papers. For a variety of reasons, the evidence as it comes from witnesses frequently differs from that appearing on the face of prosecution statements, often taken months before the trial by police officers who cannot know whether or not the story being given them is true, false or simply the best that an imperfect witness can give. If at the half-way stage in a trial when the prosecution case has been closed it becomes clear that whatever evidence has been called does not have sufficient weight for a conviction the defence can submit that there is no case to answer and hope that the trial Judge will uphold that contention. Even before that stage in a trial it sometimes happens that the Judge or prosecution counsel, having seen the primary witness's evidence fall down and there being nothing further of a really probative nature to come, will decide that the case should not go on. For whatever reason, the case against Inspector Legge ended at an early stage in the trial, effectively discharging him from the case with a not guilty verdict, leaving only Drury and Ingram remaining in the dock. Mr Legge may well have been justified in his complaint that he had been suspended from duty for longer than any other officer in the Metropolitan Police whilst awaiting his trial and he made it plain that his future lay elsewhere than in the service.

The first Crown witness was James Humphries himself. He admitted that he was currently serving a period of eight years' imprisonment in connection with a serious assault, and that in 1971/2 he was collecting £2,000 each week from his nine book shops. He paid Mr Drury £50 a week to begin with "just to keep my business running smooth and to ensure that Flying Squad officers would keep away from his premises". From August 1971 and until Drury's suspension in March 1972 the payments were increased to £100 a week, and he explained the doubling of his weekly contribution by telling the jury that he had been informed of a plot by some Senior Detectives to frame him. He had spoken to Drury about this danger and had been reassured that the matter could be dealt with, however, as events turned out, whatever efforts Drury may have made on his behalf did not result in the plot being dropped and here he was, serving a term of imprisonment for a crime he did not commit.

Mr Schindler, on behalf of Drury cross-examined Humphries on every aspect of his evidence, challenging his story of paying money to Drury and in particular the genuineness of the diary he had kept of his contact with Drury and other police officers. Humphries fielded all these questions and maintained that his diary was a true record of contacts with police officers over a long period. It was suggested to Humphries that he had two particular grudges against Drury and these grudges were behind his decision to give evidence for the Crown. First, Mr Schindler suggested that in Drury's remarks to the press about the Cyprus holiday, Drury had exposed him to *News of the World* journalists as a police informer. To a man living within or on the fringes of a heavy criminal culture, such an allegation could have fatal results. Second in importance but nonetheless undesirable was that he considered Drury had a responsibility for his present plight. Humphries's response to this was to elaborate on the plot, saying that a Superintendent, John Bland, had "framed" him as revenge for Drury having to resign from the force. In this context, he claimed that a more senior officer, a Deputy Assistant Commissioner, had been involved in the scheme to have him convicted. Name after name of allegedly corrupt officers poured from his diary in the course of his evidence and although this phase of the case came as a surprise to the public, it was not new to the Metropolitan Police Commissioner because an investigation was well under way and on June 21, 1977, whilst the trial was continuing, Deputy Assistant Commissioner Ronald Davis resigned. A few days earlier, Detective Superintendent Bland was suspended from duty and was later allowed to retire on medical grounds.

Humphries' wife June, or "Rusty" as she was better

known among the family's intimates, was called to give evidence for the prosecution and she told the jury that she had seen her husband giving money to Drury in a night club. George Schindler launched a vigorous cross-examination on Drury's behalf, implying over and over again that she was not telling the truth. However "Rusty" seems to have given as good as she got, leaving the witness box with her allegations ringing in the jury's ears.

Drury gave evidence on his own behalf and set out his perception of the Flying Squad's philosophy and practice in the use of informants. It was absolutely essential, he said, to mix socially with people connected with the criminal fraternity. "During my career I made a point of mixing with criminals. It is essential that you do so because you cannot expect them to give you information about crimes if you ostracise them except when you want information from them. It was essential that you obtained, groomed and nurtured informants continuously". That is why, he claimed, he developed a friendship with Humphries.

There were no rules about cultivating informants and when money was paid out to one of them it came from a special fund and would be signed for in a code name. He denied ever having taken any money from Humphries and where Humphries had made diary entries apparently concerning him, he did not keep many of the appointments because the man was becoming quite a nuisance. His evidence amounted to blanket denial of having received anything from Humphries which could be tainted with corruption.

The trial had lasted for three weeks and wound towards

its end with the jury having to spend a night at an hotel. On their return to court after retiring for a substantial part of a second day they pronounced verdicts of guilty to the main charges against both men and, in particular, a charge against Drury in connection with the Cyprus holiday. In passing sentence, Mr Justice Peter Payne said:

> "I find it difficult to over-estimate the seriousness of offences of this nature, most especially when they are committed by a police officer of the high rank of Commander."
>
> "If there is a lack of leadership of this kind, clearly the work of junior officers must be affected, and it must be a case of the higher the rank the greater the offence. It must not be forgotten how these offences first came to light. We owe a debt first of all to the press, for the matter of the Cyprus holiday and to Sir Robert Mark and the many officers who assisted in this investigation who pressed it relentlessly."

Drury was sentenced to six years' imprisonment with a further two years' consecutive for the Cyprus charge, a total of eight years, with an order to pay £2,000 towards his defence costs. Ingram was sent to prison for four years and ordered to pay £1,000 in costs.

Both men sought leave to appeal against their conviction on the grounds that a fair trial had been impossible in the light of adverse press and television publicity surrounding their arrests. Their application to appeal against conviction was rejected, but the Lord Chief Justice and his colleagues reduced Drury's sentence to one of five years' and Ingram's to three years'. In announcing their findings, Lord Lane said, "These two men were dazzled by the wealth of this man Humphries who was prepared, as against a rainy day, to spend as much of his money as he thought fit to keep policemen likely to cross his path sweet. The blaze of publicity that heralded Mr Drury's arrest in 1976 was regrettable and should never have happened. The screening by the BBC during the trial of a documentary on the Yard's complaints branch might have had serious consequences, but the court did not think it had."

The Humphries's diaries which had proved so devastating in the trials came under attack yet again in the Court of Appeal when Wallace Virgo appealed against his conviction. Lord Chief Justice Lane sitting with Mr Justice Thompson and Mr Justice Stephen Brown heard the appeal at the High Court on March 15, 1978, the grounds of which included a submission that the trial Judge had not dealt with Virgo's evidence in a proper way, and that the diaries had been given undue importance. The court quashed the convictions. Lord Lane, in giving the court's judgment, first praised the way in which Mr Justice Mars-Jones had presided over what had been a very difficult trial. However, he then went on to say, "A Judge was entitled to comment strongly on the evidence. It was not easy to say when the proper bounds were transgressed, but in the present case the Judge reached the limits of proper judicial comment when he said to the jury that certain of the appellants' evidence was another instance of his being caught out in a deliberate lie, and described him as 'threshing about like a fish, well and truly hooked', and, 'charging about in different directions in an effort to escape'. No injustice was caused when the remarks were weighed against the evidence to which the jury had been listening for weeks, but it was the sort of situation where a defendant left the court feeling ill-used and a butt for judicial rhetoric.

The appellant's complaint with regard to the diaries again turned upon the trial Judge's remarks to the jury. Humphries had been allowed by the Judge in giving his evidence, to refer to his own diaries as an *aide memoire*. In summing-up to the jury, the Judge made clear the law regarding corroboration generally of a man in Humphries's position as an accomplice and of bad character, doing so in a way that could not be faulted. However, in dealing with the probative value of the diaries he did not point out that, if the jury found them to be genuine, at the highest they showed a degree of consistency in Humphries's evidence. Nor did he point out that they were in no way evidence of the truth of their contents. Their Lordships decided that the jury must inevitably have been left with the impression that even if the diaries were not corroboration, they were the very next best thing.

In 1977, it was common for Judges to comment on the evidence rather than simply remind the jury of the salient points. Consider for a moment the effect of a strong commanding figure in his red robe who has controlled a long trial with a firm hand and is clearly in complete command. Consider the feeling of an average juryman or woman pitched into this strange environment and being spoon-fed information from a variety of sources over a long period. The last words they have heard, delivered by the dominant actor in the drama, come from the Judge to whom they have listened with awe and respect. Consider how potent are any opinions he has expressed in those last words, and their effect if they are unfairly biased against one side or the other. Time has moved on and such a summing-up would be unlikely today. Having said that, judicial habits die hard and it is not uncommon to hear a Judge preface a damaging personal opinion with such words as "you may think XYZ but that is a matter for you", and to accompany the remark with a sigh, despairing glance at the ceiling, or other meaningful look. Just as police officers, in spite of having presented a perfectly presented case to the prosecuting authority, exaggerate significant parts of their evidence or perjure themselves to obviate the risk of an acquittal. Juries do not always fall for this sort of thing and if they believe that they are being treated as fools, will react by acquitting defendants. It must also be admitted that modern juries have reacted against blatant attempts by a Judge to bully them into the verdict he requires and returned a perverse verdict allowing a guilty person to go free.

In addition to the appeal of Virgo, the court was also asked to reduce the sentences passed on 10 other convicted porn squad officers, ranging from three to 12 years. Lord Lane said that one turned to the cases with a heavy heart in view of the sheer waste of manpower in confining men to prison who could make a contribution to society. But for years that section of the Metropolitan Police had been involved in wholesale corruption. The very men employed to bring the corrupt to book were thriving on the proceeds of corruption. It was the unpleasant task of the court to ensure that the level of sentence in cases like the present was sufficient to provide the stimulus to the faint-hearted to avoid becoming involved. Heavy sentences were undoubtedly called for. The overall level of sentence was correct, and the individual sentences properly reflected the degree of complicity and wickedness.

So ended the series of devastating trials, leaving the Metropolitan Police to lick its wounds and begin the task of regaining public confidence.

Chapter 9

Some Personal Remembrances

In the course of this study, incidents of bribery and corruption have been of such long-standing that the mechanism of their beginnings has been long forgotten. It may be of interest therefore to look at some personal experience of approaches which, had they been encouraged, could so easily have led to criminal misbehaviour of the kind under review. It is said that every man has his price but I like to believe that it was a strong moral revulsion that saved me from such temptations. But who can be sure of themselves if the price is sufficiently high?

During the late 1960s I had occasion to meet a known criminal in a pub, where he was supposed to give me information about a burglary of a jeweller's shop from which a substantial amount of stock had been stolen. We were convinced that it was an inside job, committed with the manager's connivance. In the absence of information, inquiries ground to a halt and the matter was going to be filed unless and until something turned up. Something did turn up, in the form of a telephone call from an active thief, unknown in our part of the world, but who was willing to pass on information. Arrangements were made for a meeting, and having had a look at his criminal record it was difficult to understand what he had to gain from it. On the face of things, there seemed to be no reason why such a man would want to become an informer because none of the usual motives seemed to fit, but within minutes of our meeting I began to suspect that he had himself taken an active part in the crime and was trying to make some kind of deal.

We sat in the bar and I paid for a round of drinks whilst our conversation ranged over various topics before the first gentle probes at the real issues began. Why did he really set this meeting up, what did he want from it, and how would it help me in my inquiries? He paid for another round of drinks with a large value note which represented more than my week's wages and left the change on the counter between us, gradually edging it nearer to me where it remained until I decided that there was no further point in the meeting. "Don't forget your change", he said as I made my farewells. The barman must have been more than a little surprised to see two customers arguing politely about who owned the change but there it stayed on the counter, at least until I went through the doors.

My colleagues and I arrested him a few days later in possession of jewellery from the shop, and charged him with handling stolen property. In spite of his unsubtle attempt at corruption, for that is what he must surely have intended, we had a guarded but amiable relationship, extending even into the days beyond his imprisonment. His motives for trying it on were never put into words but one has often wondered what might have happened had I been foolish enough to swallow the bait and pick up those few pounds.

A more serious attempt arose out of an inquiry into the activities of a fraudulent estate agent and a solicitor with whom he operated. In the early 1970s, inflation and other economic factors were pushing up housing costs in the south of England to an alarming level with prices being increased almost daily. Gazumping was the name of the game with vendors accepting offers on their property and then pushing the price up when another prospective purchaser came on the scene. This particular agent operated in a district where most houses were small terraced properties, formerly workmen's cottages built to house men and their families employed in local breweries and on the busy railway. Built in the late 19th century they were, typically, two bedroom dwellings with a parlour, tiny dining room and minuscule kitchen. Those with bathrooms had sacrificed one of the bedrooms for the purpose and were, in spite of their restricted accommodation, particularly attractive to young people as their first home. Into this environment stepped the agent, a man in his middle years, an undischarged bankrupt with a conviction for fraud.

He seemed to have lost control of his accounting rather than having started on a deliberate course of fraud, but in a very short time old habits had resurfaced and he began spending the deposit moneys entrusted to him by hopeful purchasers. In a vain attempt to keep the ball rolling along and replace the money he had used, he hit on the idea of holding two or more deposits on individual properties until he had amassed some surplus from legitimate transactions to cover the shortages. By the time one young couple who had been promised completion on their future home lost patience and begun to ask questions, there were as many as six others with deposits laid down on the same property and most of it lost forever.

Part of the deal he offered to clients was the opportunity to use a solicitor with whom he was on good terms, who would guarantee prompt legal services at reasonable cost. This was an attractive offer to first-time buyers with no experience of house buying and, in many of the transactions, this offer was taken up with gratitude. The solicitor, a man of considerable experience with a lucrative London practice, would come to the estate agency on Saturday mornings when he would interview clients and prepare all the necessary documents for their purchase. The sales office was housed in a dingy room facing a run-down street and buyers who decided to use the "in house" legal services, would be ushered into a back office where the solicitor held court. It was inconceivable that he did not become aware of the financial problems looming up on the business and certain it was that he was aware of the agent's status as an undischarged bankrupt. He was also admittedly aware that the business was a limited company and that its principal director was the agent, an office from which he was barred under the criminal law.

Both were arrested and the tedious task of collecting evidence of multiple frauds began. It was during the period when these inquiries were under way that a gentleman who contacted me in the capacity of the solicitor's representative asked for a meeting in order to discuss the timetable and other matters connected with the forthcoming trial. As a courtesy I met him at the railway station and, when our meeting ended, took him back to catch the London train. He was an amiable and articulate man nearing his 70s whose object was to offer help in smoothing the course of our inquiries, and in doing so, to see how far I might be inclined to play down his client's culpability in my approach to the case. After a polite but firm refusal, graciously accepted, our business was concluded. On the way back to the station and over a cup of coffee our conversation ranged over a number of topics including his past history and my leisure activities. He had been a solicitor and city councillor in South Africa but had felt obliged to leave under political pressure. Unqualified as an advocate in England and of retiring age, he was passing a little time helping and advising, as a friend, the solicitor with whom I was concerned.

One of our neutral topics was my then interest in fly fishing, a subject of which he knew a little, and of sailing a very small dinghy with my children on a local lake. I had to confess that I had never fished for salmon, nor could I ever imagine being able to afford to do so. When he returned to the topic of sailing I admitted that a larger class of dinghy might well be in my sights within a year or so, but for the present I would make do with what I had and with that we parted until our next meeting in a weeks' time.

It was only a few days later that he was on the telephone to invite me to somewhere close to the River Wye, where he had a friend with a beat on the river and who wished to invite us both down for a weekend's fishing. Next it was yet another friend who would be overjoyed to arrange some special deal for me on a sailing boat worth about four times as much as my modest little craft. Were they laughably naive attempts to get me to accept favours with no strings attached? Or were they the opening moves in a much deeper game to compromise the investigator in order to get a defendant off a very sharp hook. It does not take a great deal of imagination to foresee what might have followed had I been foolish enough to take up either offer. It may be, however, that there was an element of naivety in the man's efforts to get a degree of sympathy for his client because some year or so later, when both defendants were nearing the end of their sentences, I had a further request for help from him. This time it was suggested that I might write to the Law Society, giving a character reference for the solicitor who had quite understandably been struck off the roll and was now seeking readmission. On this occasion there were no promises of material benefit, but simply an appeal to my good nature, which he had grossly over-estimated.

I am quite sure that many of my colleagues must have experienced similar attempts to divert them from their duty but it is a curious fact that none of them ever mentioned such things to me, even when I was their immediate superior. Perhaps their thinking ran along the lines that if it is not talked about it will disappear?

The criminal bar is organised in such a way that defending barristers are, in the main, paid from government funds through the legal aid system although there are many occasions when a defendant must fund his own representation. In either case there is a solicitor standing between client and counsel, who is responsible for setting fees and, in privately funded matters, collecting those fees and paying them over. There is no scope so far as I have been able to discover in which corruption could profit any party to the matter in hand. That did not prevent one young gentleman from testing the water when I saw him in conference. He had been arrested driving a Ferrari sports car at 70 mph along Park Lane and, when stopped and tested for alcohol, was well over the limit and, as an Iranian Moslem, he was in difficulties with his father with regard to his drinking and even more with the forthcoming court appearance.

We went over the evidence together and it became clear that he had no defence to an excess alcohol charge and speeding. There was no way in which a court could be persuaded not to disqualify him from driving, even a brand new Ferrari, but this was advice he found hard to accept and tried to explore with me some means of changing the evidence. Eventually he got around to asking outright if there was a way in which the two policemen who had arrested him could be bought off. The solicitor who accompanied him raised his eyes to heaven and ushered him rapidly out of my chambers.

There were many occasions when I was offered "a drink" if I did a good job for a client. These were usually thieves and vagabonds at the lower end of criminal activity and it was of no use to tell them that they would be properly represented, who or whatever they were. Often too, when they had been acquitted, there would be a grateful promise of a bottle of brandy which would be delivered to my chambers without fail. Had those bottles materialised, I could have set up an off-licence. There was one memorable "drink"left for me in chambers and it came from a Nigerian minor royal whose daughter was due in court next day to be sentenced for issuing a dud cheque. The amount was small and she was a student without previous convictions, making the likely sentence a stiff fine. So it proved. I had no qualms about accepting this gift in the circumstances, which turned out to be a beautifully presented bottle of champagne and two glasses, all exquisitely hand painted. And it was good champagne!

Chapter 10

Outside the Met

All the instances of major corruption covered so far in this book have involved the Metropolitan Police and it would be wrong to assume that it alone had been subject to such problems, because every police service, large or small, has suffered in some measure. Those forces which are responsible for mainly rural areas have escaped, not necessarily because their personnel are incorruptible, but because there is little scope for much more than being paid to "forget" a traffic violation or something similar within their environment. Indeed, whenever there have been dishonest practices in police services within the Commonwealth, Metropolitan officers have been among those sent abroad to help solve the problems. Nor has that assistance always been confined to the Commonwealth for as far back as 1860, Chief Inspector Jonathan Whicher was seconded from Scotland Yard to Poland at its government's request, in an attempt to instil some of the British ideals into their police system. That it was unsuccessful was no fault of the British system, nor of the officer who had been given what was quickly realised to be an impossible task, but to an unbridgeable gap in the different cultures.

During the late 1960s and early 70s, it was a combined group of Metropolitan and provincial officers who were sent to Hong Kong to combat a deeply embedded system of corruption within the Royal Hong Kong Police involving a number of both European and ethnic Chinese personnel. Most recently it has been a senior officer, Mr Peter Ryan, formerly Commandant of the Bramshill Police College who now, as Commissioner of Police, is turning the New South

Wales Police from having the reputation of being the most corrupt force in Australia to being as honest as any. The need to bring that new broom into the NSW police will be explored in the next chapters, but in case anyone should run away with the notion that it is only services with their roots in the UK tradition of citizen policemen that may be corrupt, a brief look at some recent press reports will show how wrong that is.

The International Herald Tribune, in a recent article referred to the Los Angeles Police in the following way. "So many lies, false arrests, dirty cops and wrongful convictions are being exposed in this latest scandal engulfing this city's police that it is getting hard to keep up with the corruption. The police chief now says that rogue officers in a neighbourhood overrun with gangs framed at least 89 people in the last three years by planting drugs or guns on them, and also may have revelled in shooting a few unarmed suspects". The District Attorney reported that 32 criminal convictions had been overturned and 20 officers had been dismissed, suspended or had resigned. "It is one of the most corrosive police corruption cases ever in Los Angeles".

In 1999, *The Daily Telegraph* published an article from their correspondent in Mexico City reporting that a Police Chief had banned all male police officers from issuing traffic violation tickets to motorists. A practice had grown up where officers would stop motorists and offer them a ticket or the alternative of paying a lesser amount, in cash, on the spot. The 900 traffic officers would still have the power to stop offending motorists, but only a special force of 22 police cars, manned by women officers, would be able to issue violation tickets. Women officers, he claimed, were less likely to open themselves to corruption than their male counterparts.

The Chief of Police in Lima, Peru, reported that since employing an all-woman unit in a similar capacity, the level of corruption had dropped sharply. "The women are more honest than the men. The male officers were only interested in collecting money to buy lunch. The women seem more concerned with doing the job", he told the press.

The New York City Police has for many years suffered from massive corruption which successive Mayors and Police Chiefs have tackled with varying degrees of success. There have been many Commissions and inquiries into the scope and causes of the problem, the latest of these being under Commissioner M. Mollen in 1994. A worthwhile review of major American police departments is far beyond the scope of this book, but in the smaller local departments, sometimes with a total of manpower of a dozen or so, there are many recorded instances of corrupt practices, often unbelievably transparent.

In browsing the internet for examples of corruption, one can find short-lived web-sites in which irate citizens try to get the world interested in their complaints against the police, generally in connection with traffic violations. Some seem to have a more solid basis of which the following is an example. Whilst one cannot verify the details of information gained from such a source, it describes what happened in one small US town. This particular item was published on the net by an aggrieved patrolman, Guy Emerson, in the police department of a small east coast town. The town was governed by a group of elected representatives known as "selectmen", roughly the equivalent of councillors, but in overall control was a "Town Manager" who had the power to engage and dismiss staff, including the police.

The patrolman detailed a list of instances in which he claimed that the Police Chief had acted corruptly by perverting the course of justice, mainly for the benefit of his family and friends. The complaint, containing a number of specific incidents, was investigated by the Town Manager and in May 1998, he wrote to the Chief of Police, dismissing him with immediate effect, specifying the following reasons:

*November 1997, your son D's hunting violation, the manner in which it was mishandled and the failure to follow up the same, based on his relationship to you;

*April 1994, the CAC automobile accident in which poor, even suspect, police work was allowed to stand in a serious auto accident based on her sister's relationship to you;

*Employing your son D as a police officer without a driver's licence;

*July 1988, incident involving your son J. jnr, who was stopped for various moving vehicle violations on his motorcycle and allowed to depart without arrest or summons, based upon his relationship to you;

* Your son D's OUI (a drink/drive offence) stop without arrest or summons, based upon his relationship to you.

The letter continued with other instances, rounded up by his "failure to carry out the duties and responsibilities of his job" and, although this decision was approved by a substantial majority of the selectmen, the Chief began an action for damages against them. By December of that year, the selectmen caved in on the basis that to fight the matter through the courts would be too expensive and they therefore settled with him for $55,000. At about the same time as the Chief was dismissed, the selectmen rewarded the patrolman for his whistleblowing by sacking him too. Unsurprisingly, he sued the Town Manager and the selectmen; had his sacking reversed and was awarded $55,000 in damages then resigned immediately from a job which would have been exceedingly uncomfortable in the future.

Chapter 11

London's "Rotten Apple"

The tenure of office of many former Commissioners of the Metropolitan police have been marred by problems such as those described earlier in this book; these and other scandals have brought sections of the press, reinforced by some politicians, to demand their resignation. Various far out pressure groups have bayed for the blood, not only of the Commissioner, but also that of the Home Secretary of the day. Every Commissioner has tried to prevent a repetition of whatever tribulations have fallen upon him and his staff, with variable determination and often limited success. Some have made little impact, but even the most innovative and robust have been able to achieve only short-term improvement. Sir Paul Condon, who retired as Commissioner in January 2000 after seven years' service was interviewed for *The Daily Telegraph* shortly before leaving, when he recalled some of the successes of his years in the office. He hoped that he would be remembered for those successes and not just the tragedy of the Lawrence case in which a black youth was murdered by a group of white hooligans who may never now be brought to account.

Sir Paul faced massive attacks as a result of that murder, not only from the predictable sources who are always ready to denigrate the police, but also from people of the highest intelligence and integrity. He found himself condemned as being in command of an "institutionally racist" body of officers, a phrase which will go down in the history of policing and race relations for many years to come. One can imagine him breathing a huge sigh of relief on closing his office door for the very last time.

In the article, he identified the campaign to root out some of the worst corruption since the seventies. Corruption, he said, was not as widespread as in the sixties but was nevertheless a serious problem. Without criticising his predecessors, he said the Met had "taken its eye off the ball" as far as the corrupting influence of drugs money was concerned.

Scotland Yard is currently spending up to £20 million a year on CIB3, a 200-strong Squad set up to investigate allegations against serving and former officers. Sir Paul denied his policy of reducing supervisory ranks had allowed corrupt officers to operate unchecked. Corruption, he said, was about opportunity and human frailty.

More than 100 people are either facing charges or are suspended, but Sir Paul said that the success of the anti-corruption campaign should not be judged by the number of convictions alone.

"The test of success is not just about numbers. It's about confidence in what we have got in place and what people believe about the process". Part of the challenge of the campaign, he said, was that the ordinary officer in police stations didn't recognise corruption there - "it is language they don't understand" - and it took some time to persuade them there was a problem.

Under his leadership, an Anti-corruption Squad (CIB3) was formed in January 1998, with a complement of 180 police officers and 32 civilian staff with a budget of £11.5 million. In an internet publication set out in the form of hypothetical questions and their answers, the question is posed:

"Is it true that the Commissioner has said that there are 250 corrupt officers in the Metropolitan Police?"

On December 4, 1997, the Home Affairs Committee asked the Commissioner, "would you give any sort of percentage to the rotten apples who should be thrown out?"

In his answer, he said, "I actually believe that we have the most honest big city police service anywhere in the world and that is the view that has been reinforced by diplomats who live and work in London. I am very proud of the majority of my men and women who serve in the Met. I would hope and believe that it contained somewhere between 100 officers and 250 officers. The media picked up on the higher figure when in fact, experience and current intelligence suggest the real numbers are closer to the 100."

Later in the website the topic of informing on one's colleagues, a matter of major concern among officers, is canvassed by the hypothetical question and answer device:

Q. "If there is corruption in the Met, how come I haven't seen it?"

A. "There are several issues here: First, the number of corrupt individuals in the Met is relatively small. Secondly, their activities are generally kept hidden from honest officers. Thirdly, honest colleagues must be aware that corruption exists before the signs and symptoms can be detected. A maxim could be that, 'if you don't know it's there you are unlikely to notice it. If you don't notice it you won't be attuned to deal with it.' The point is if you did see or hear something that caused you unease, did you report it to someone who could take action about it? If you didn't, why not? You have a duty to report corrupt behaviour and we would wish to reassure you that people who do will be treated fairly, sympathetically and responsibly by the MPS [Metropolitan Police Service - the former title using the word Force has been dropped in favour of Service]. If an investigation reveals that you made an honest mistake, then neither you nor, of course, the person you had concerns about will be penalised. We recognise that this is another very difficult and sometimes distressing area for MPS staff to confront. However, turning a blind eye to corruption is actually part of the problem because corruption will continue unchecked if it is ignored. It will take courage for you to come forward, but you can have faith that the MPS can and will support you when you do."

Q. "Would an officer be in jeopardy if he or she saw something and didn't report it?"

A. "Possibly, yes. Certain criminal and disciplinary offences are committed, depending on the circumstances. For example, the Police (Misconduct) Regulations introduced in April 1999, state '... Officers should support their colleagues in the execution of their lawful duties, and oppose any improper behaviour, reporting it where appropriate ...'. As already mentioned, corruption will carry on unchecked if people ignore it so we must ensure that colleagues don't ignore it. If you know about

> corruption which you didn't report in the past, we recognise this may be worrying you. The Deputy Commissioner has approved an 'amnesty from discipline' in certain circumstances to encourage otherwise worried staff to come forward and tell us about it."

These questions and answers set out a straightforward philosophy to which all honest members of the service would hopefully subscribe, and put the position of the informer fair and square in his or her relationship *vis-à-vis* management. They do not, however, offer comfort to those who are concerned about the reaction of their colleagues generally to the "whistleblower". That reaction can be bitter and long lasting regardless of how honest and public spirited the individual.

Sir Paul Condon was still Commissioner in October when this document was put on the website and barely a month later, another corruption prosecution began against a group of officers from a unit of the Regional Crime Squad.

Detective Constable Bob Clark, Detective Sergeant Chris Drury, Detective Constable Neill Putnam, Detective Constable Thomas Kingston, and Detective Constable Thomas Reynolds, appeared at the Central Criminal Court charged in an indictment alleging conspiracy to supply drugs and perverting the course of justice. Charged with them was a woman, Evelyn Fleckney. The men had all been members of the East Dulwich Regional Crime Squad when Clark was instructed to act as "handler" to Evelyn Fleckney, a major drugs dealer who had turned informer. Her information was so valuable that Clark's success rate in arresting drugs dealers increased dramatically until she herself, in 1998, was sentenced to 15 years' imprisonment and informed on Clark's activities. It was largely as a result of her information that CB3's investigations bore fruit, leading to the trial of the whole group.

Putnam elected to plead guilty to the main charge, as did Evelyn Fleckney and they both elected to give evidence against the remainder of those charged with them. Before the contested part of the case began, Putnam was sentenced to three years 11 months imprisonment, and Fleckney to four years six months, to be served concurrently with the 15-year sentence. In passing those sentences the Judge's comments were as scathing as those of the Judge in the 1977 trials. Mr Justice Blofeld said:

> "If an élite squad, which is there to catch the most sophisticated criminals who sadly abound in our society, turns to crime, then their whole efforts are aborted and society suffers. The squad was not well run. Your supervision was not what it should have been. Your superiors were not themselves adequately supervised. At times, the approach of the squad was that they could do as they wanted. You fell in with that."

The pattern of the team's offending was depressingly familiar. According to Putnam's evidence they would target drugs dealers and instead of dealing properly with drugs they seized from them, would sell them to other dealers. Their profits from this activity were so great that Clark, who had formed an intimate relationship with Fleckney was able to spend nights with her at expensive London hotels, take her on foreign holidays and buy her expensive presents. Clark, formerly a member of the Flying Squad, received a sentence of 12 years; Drury was sentenced to 11 years; Kingston and Reynolds, for stealing and selling amphetamines, received three years and six months each. Putnam, for acts intended to pervert the course of justice by falsifying a report, was sentenced to two years.

Mr Justice Blofeld, passing sentence on Clark and Drury said, "I do not consider the primary motive for either of you was personal gain but power. Both of you by your behaviour displayed a considerable degree of arrogance. Both of you took the view that the law was for lesser mortals than you. You did whatever you wanted whether it was inside or outside the law".

In March 2000, CIB3 itself came under heavy criticism in a Sunday newspaper which ran an article on a number of Flying Squad officers who had been investigated by the branch. Two of them had spent time in custody awaiting trial before being acquitted at the Central Criminal Court; two others had been suspended for a considerable time before their cases were dismissed by a magistrate who refused to commit them for trial. At the Central Criminal Court, the Judge withdrew the case from the jury after 11 weeks of legal argument based, in part, on the admissibility of some prosecution evidence, breaches of court rulings by the Criminal Prosecution Service which failed to release documents as ordered, and oppressive behaviour by investigators. Not a word of evidence was heard by the jury in all that time and one cannot help but wonder how a situation like this was possible, considering the resources available to the prosecution with experienced investigators and lawyers skilled in criminal law and procedures.

In defence of this debacle, Deputy Assistant Commissioner Roy Clark said:

> "The overwhelming majority of police officers know they have nothing to fear from CIB. The methods and tactics we use have been made known through seminars and internal publications. Over 96% fully support and endorse what CIB are doing, as do the Police Federation who speak at the seminars. The techniques we use are lawful and ethical. The public deserve and expect an honest police service and our strategy ensures they get it."

Predictably, politicians were invited to give their views on the case and the Shadow Home Secretary said, "With a budget of £11.5 millions a year and over 180 officers it does seem extraordinary there have only been eight convictions", whilst a back bench member on the government's side weighed in with a call for an inquiry into CIB3 by a Judge and independent police force. Chief officers and Ministers have learned that with regard to corruption, they are damned if they do, and damned if they don't, do something about it. And when their efforts fail, they are thrice damned.

New South Wales Police
Australia

and

The Royal Commission Report
Into the New South Wales
Police Service

Chapter 12

Origins of the Problem

In 1770, Captain James Cook landed briefly on a beach which would become known as Botany Bay, but his stay was only of sufficient time to make a cursory study of the very edge of an enormous land mass which would in due time be named Australia. On his return to England with a log of the journey, his description of this new land was of a green and fertile place, ideally suitable for colonisation and able to support a community of farming settlers. Some 15 or so years later, at a time when crime in England was out of control and its prisons so overcrowded that many convicts were obliged to serve out their time within the confines of rotting hulks in which disease became rife, there was no question of rehabilitation being part of punishment philosophy, and it was almost inevitable that those who completed their sentence would soon be back. In a society that tolerated hanging as suitable punishment for felony, which included minor thefts, coining, forgery and other crimes, severe punishment was thought to be the only way to exercise a measure of deterrence. When the idea of banishing convicts from the country first dawned on the official mind, the attraction of disposing of those regarded as human waste became obvious. To get rid of them to Virginia and, later, this new and wonderful land, had a further benefit in that there would be a plentiful supply of tied labour at the disposal of emigrant settlers at very little cost. One small example may help to illustrate how severe a punishment transportation was; a man was transported for life having stolen 12 yards of lace and a pair of lady's stockings. Seven years was the minimum term, but as we shall see, this could be extended at the whim of a master. The new land of Australia was the obvious place to condemn such heinous villains to years of slavery and hardship.

In January 1787, a melancholy cargo of over 500 men and almost 200 women convicted of such crimes, aboard 11 ships of the First Fleet under the command of Captain Arthur Philip, arrived in Sydney Cove. Apart from the ships' crew, there were Marine guards whose task was to keep order and prevent mutiny during the months of long passage from England, and because there was no police organisation awaiting the immigrants, to continue in that role ashore for some time to come.

Apart from those of education and good background who had fallen into crime, most convicts had suffered hardship and brutality in their native land, but it was as nothing to what would follow for many of them in the early years as they served out their sentence. Flogging was the first thought in the minds of sadistic magistrates before whom convicts were brought and it was commonplace for a man or woman to be awarded 50 strokes of the cat for such misconduct as insubordination to their master. The magistrates appeared to support the practice of some masters, who would trump up some minor charge against a convict worker nearing the end of his or her sentence, so that release from bondage by the grant of a ticket of leave was delayed for a further long period. Hanging was common for those convicted of more serious crimes, although landowners were reluctant to lose a useful slave to the gallows unless he was of such character as to present a danger to them. The more usual candidates for the hangman were bushrangers - those escaped convicts who preferred to live in the wilds by means of theft and robbery as an alternative to the hard labour and harsh discipline of servitude. Bushrangers flourished in Tasmania and in New South Wales from the turn of the century, first as a relatively rare phenomenon but later in increasing numbers; however, by 1839, they existed only in places beyond the range of the mounted police.

Regardless of their surviving by stealing, even from those with property barely worth taking, they were not as badly thought of as were the police in the eyes of emancipated prisoners, fugitives from the law and free emigrant settlers. The police were regarded as brutal and bullying, not only towards their captives, but also to innocent farmers and traders whom they suspected of helping the bushrangers. It may be that they had some reason for irritation, because it was not unknown for a smallholder to buy stolen sheep from the bushrangers with no questions asked. It is this familiarity and guarded sympathy existing between them and the rural population, that spawned ballads such as *The Wild Colonial Boy* and *Bold Jack Donahue*, still sung at folk music sessions in Australia, Ireland and those bars in the USA frequented by nostalgic Americans boasting the merest hint of Irish ancestry.

They were a target for the Military Mounted Police and the Border Police, two separate groups who, jealous of each other, were in constant conflict. Within Sydney, policing was carried out by convict watchmen or constables with little or no training in their functions and who were prone to forget such foolish notions of duty when personal profit was there for the taking.

The Sydney Police Act 1833, provided the start of a more formal police organisation, staffed by some former police officers from the mother country, ex-soldiers and marines together with supposedly trustworthy time expired convicts. Such was the frontier environment in which the new police were obliged to operate, that their effectiveness was patchy and their commitment and integrity more so. There must have been many among them who believed in right and justice and in consequence did their best to uphold it, but there were many others who saw the opportunity for personal gain arising from their position of power, and seized it however questionable the method. Most of their senior officers were in no position to control the constable's illegal activities because they themselves were engaging in schemes of doubtful honesty, evidenced by the fact that several of the first chief officers were dismissed for misbehaviour of one kind or another.

Over a period, the service developed along similar lines to that in England with a gradual shift to the creation of specialist departments, starting with a Detective group whose members, unconsciously following the pattern of Scotland Yard's Detectives, rapidly acquired a taste for the delights of élitism. Whilst the "ordinary" police had only limited opportunity for serious corruption, because of a wide range of duties within their responsibility, Detectives had more serious kinds of criminal activity to deal with and were subjected to those temptations that surround serious crime and criminals. Although there were similar police developments taking place in England and Australia, one must look at them in the light of radical differences in their populations. Whilst England's population was made up of people from all walks of life with centuries of history and culture behind them, Australia's newly transplanted population consisted of a military and civil service administration, a body of serving and freed criminals, and emigrants taking the enormous step of seeking a new life in a (to them) virtually unknown environment.

Suspicions of corruption surrounded the police from the earliest times but it was not until 1867 that the first official inquiry was set in motion to examine complaints of police misconduct in New South Wales. It was suspected that some officers were in league with criminals, whilst others, through inefficiency and inexperience, were simply allowing them to operate undisturbed. The Commissioners appointed to carry out the inquiry came to the conclusion that there had been improper intimacy between members of the force and associates of the bushrangers, putting the blame firmly upon the Superintendent in charge of the particular district under examination. The situation could not have existed, they reported, had he exercised strict and proper control over his men. How many times since, one must ask rhetorically, have similar conclusions been reached by those investigating complaints of impropriety among police officers?

Over the next 100 years there were many official inquiries into aspects of alleged corruption in such activities as gambling, prostitution, robbery and illegal supply of liquor, but it is in the last decade of the 20th century that matters of greatest interest within the context of this book arose, in particular events recorded in the 1997 Royal

Commission's report into the New South Wales Police Service, by the Hon. Justice J.R.T. Wood, and the conclusions reached at the end of an exhaustive investigation.

There have already been a number of Commissions of Inquiry and the public perception of the NSW police was of a thoroughly corrupt and dishonest body of men and women, who were not to be trusted and could command little respect, even among the most law-abiding citizens who, in other jurisdictions, would be the first to support them. So great was the disquiet among ordinary people, the press and some senior politicians, that appointment of a Royal Commission became inevitable even in the face of objections from those who complained that the inquiry was a waste of time and money. To break down those barriers which are usually thrown up when a potentially damaging inquiry is set on foot, the Commission was given unusually wide powers, including the ability to grant conditional immunity to offenders and witnesses. Some investigators were brought in from outside the NSW police and closely vetted to ensure total integrity and an absence of any links to possible suspects within the service or its staff. They were given power to obtain and execute search warrants, arrest and interrogate suspects and to set up electronic surveillance systems on suspected officers and their civilian associates. Evidence before the Commission was taken on oath and examination of those appearing before it either as witnesses or suspects was undertaken by senior counsel. The success of the Commission can be judged by its report and by subsequent events.

It will no doubt be noticed as this look at the NSW police

progresses that there are remarkable similarities between that organisation's problems and those of the Metropolitan police, both in the relative time-scales and the nature of officers' misuse of their powers. However, there will also be noted substantial differences which render some comparisons between the two unreliable. A similarity can be seen in the "firm within a firm" situation where squads, rotten to the core, were able to investigate themselves and present a clean bill of health to the world at large. A major difference can be seen in that a number of corrupt Met officers were eventually exposed to the full light of criminal trials as the preferred solution, whilst corrupt NSW officers were much more likely to face an inquiry within the legal system, but with dismissal as a more likely outcome. The decision to grant amnesty to officers who had been found to be seriously corrupt caused a great deal of disquiet in the press and an inevitable outcry from the public; although many officers were prosecuted, many more were simply allowed to leave without fuss on the basis that too many prosecutions would clog the legal system for a long time. There was probably an undisclosed economic item on the agenda too, because in 1998, the then Director of Public Prosecutions was complaining that his department was overworked and underfunded for the task. Whether London's punitive approach was more effective than Sydney's pragmatic, is for the reader to judge.

Chapter 13

Conception of the Royal Commission in 1994

The Royal Commission was conceived in May 1994 during three stormy days in the NSW Parliament when Mr John Hatton, a South Coast Independent member, made a series of allegations against senior officers of the NSW police and others, accusing them of corruption on a grand scale and demanding that a Royal Commission be appointed. He had been campaigning for reform of the police for 20 years with some successes, but now, the allegations he put in a speech to Parliament were so serious and far reaching that, with great reluctance and only after the Independent members joined with the Opposition, the government was forced to concede to his demand.

So serious was the level of corruption in public life generally that there was a Commission already in existence, the Independent Commission against Corruption (ICAC), created and empowered by the Independent Commission against Corruption Act 1988. Its purpose was to target corruption within the public sector including the police service and it had achieved some limited success in dealing with many complaints against the police, but was accused of having neither sufficient enthusiasm nor resources to take on the wide-ranging and serious problems raised by Hatton. The acting head of the ICAC, Mr John Mant, rejected these claims but, significantly, complained of the government's delay in appointing a full-time Commissioner to replace Mr Ian Tenby, QC, who had completed his five-year term some months earlier. He asserted that the restructuring of the Commission and deciding on future policy was outside the proper terms of reference for an Acting Commissioner and, referring to the paedophile inquiry his office had been asked to undertake, said that the Government should properly equip the Commission to deal with it. The Government's response to Mr Mant's complaints were that the selection and appointment of a new Commissioner was a lengthy and complicated task.

The Government, pressed by Mr Hatton for a Royal Commission to be set up, responded by claiming that the ICAC was the appropriate body to look into matters, but it must have been fully aware of the severe limitations under which that body was already working. In the days following the MP's revelations, a number of people protested long and loud that the ICAC should be allowed to undertake the inquiry into police corruption which it had in some particular aspects already begun. Among the early objectors was the Premier, Mr Fahey, who argued that the proper body to deal with the revelations was the ICAC, but after two other Independent members, Mr Clover Moore and Dr Peter Macdonald joined with the Opposition in supporting Hatton's demands, Mr Fahey conceded and put his support behind the new Commission.

Mr Hatton named senior police officers or former officers in his speech including the then Commissioner, three Assistant Commissioners, a former Assistant Commissioner and a number of Superintendents, saying that he had serious concerns about their honesty and or competence. He went on to say that a further 23 serving and former police officers had come to "adverse notice" in an intelligence investigation into allegations of heroin trafficking and links with murder, money laundering and other serious crimes. Two of those he named in this context were Assistant Commissioners. Mr Hatton told Parliament that he was in possession of a signed statement from a former police officer who claimed that he had, in 1979 and under orders, run a surveillance operation on the then Attorney General, Frank Walker, but without anything detrimental being found. After describing police surveillance of other MPs on the orders of an Assistant Commissioner, Hatton told the House, "This is chilling evidence that senior police in NSW are prepared to put Members of Parliament under surveillance for what appears to be no other purpose than to collect intelligence". He then went on to name an officer who had leaked information about a top-level internal inquiry into police corruption, thus compromising its effectiveness. He also drew attention to specific instances of unfair treatment meted out to officers who had been sufficiently unwise as to protest about corruption: the pejoratively dubbed "whistleblowers".

Once Parliament had decided to set up the Royal Commission, events moved remarkably quickly, beginning with the appointment as Commissioner of Justice James Wood, a 53-year old Queen's Counsel who had been a Supreme Court Justice for 10 years. His terms of reference, set out by the Premier in the House, included investigating the nature and extent of corruption in the police force, police internal investigations, the system of promotions in the service, the impartiality of police in pursuing prosecutions including paedophile activity, the internal informer's policy, and any other matter concerning possible criminal activity, neglect or violation of duty considered to be against the public interest. These terms of reference were very wide and left scope for the Commission to look at various peripheral matters if it seemed necessary. In November 1994, Assent was given to the Royal Commission (Police Service) Act 1994, which gave statutory authority to the work already begun in midsummer of that year.

It was not only the Premier whose preference was for the matter to be dealt with by the ICAC, but whilst he was ultimately obliged to capitulate, others maintained their objection, often unwisely and always vociferously. Under *The Sydney Morning Herald* headline LAUER SCORNS HATTON CLAIMS, the Police Commissioner, Tony Lauer, dismissed suggestions of entrenched corruption in his force as "figments of political imagination", a contention which could hardly have been farther from reality as events began to unfold. Minister for Police, Terry Griffiths, supported Mr Lauer's statement that they believed the majority of police officers to be honest, adding that the Royal Commission was as much about the "credibility of the accusers as the accused". Mr Lauer took further exception to the Royal Commission on the grounds that it would tie up police resources in gathering material for the Commission and he himself would be tied up for years. Once the Commission was appointed however, Lauer issued orders to the force to co-operate fully with the Commission's requests and, in particular, to refrain from the normal routine of destroying redundant reports and papers which might be needed in the inquiry.

The Police Association, the representative body for junior officers and very much in the nature of a police trades union, came out strongly in opposition to the Royal

Commission at a meeting on May 13, attended by about 100 branch members who voiced their support for Mr Lauer. The Deputy President of the Association, Mr Terry O'Connell, told the meeting that the union could not support the Royal Commission. He went on to explain that the members were not scared of the prospect, but that there was already an investigating body, the ICAC, capable of carrying out the inquiry and that the State would be better served by leaving it to them. It is against this background of opposition that the Royal Commission began its daunting task of breaking through the hard shell of what was perceived to be an organisation riddled from the highest levels with dishonesty and incompetence.

In the course of the inquiry, many officers were questioned, on oath and in depth about their own or their colleagues' integrity. Some had been questioned in the course of earlier investigations and their statements made at that time were frequently available to the Wood Commission investigators who, comparing those with the officer's present answers, discovered serious discrepancies. Determined effort were made to "turn" those who were clearly involved in corrupt practices, to persuade them to co-operate with the Commission and help break through the wall of silence. One of the most powerful weapons provided for the Commission and its investigators was the power to recommend an amnesty in suitable cases. The amnesty was announced with the approval of the Government, supported by the Opposition and police associations, to the effect that it was open only until February 9, 1996, a period of 70 days. For any officer who was prepared to acknowledge his or her part in unlawful practices and apply for amnesty, there were conditions:

> There must be a full and frank admission of their corrupt activities.
> There must be a full account of their knowledge of corrupt activities.
> Unconditional notice of resignation from the service must be received before the cut-off date.

In the offer of amnesty, it was spelled out in no nonsense terms that corrupt officers who decided to "tough it out" might find themselves prosecuted, based upon what their contemporaries might reveal in their own claims for amnesty. The weapon proved to be exceedingly potent, because during the Commission's inquiries into the Physical Surveillance Branch, 28 of its members seized the opportunity presented by the amnesty and resigned from the force.

Before turning to specific areas where corruption was thought to exist, one should mention that an investigation into paedophile activities as they affected the police service had already begun by the ICAC. This aspect of the problem was turned over to the Wood Commission who found a disturbing picture of neglect, indifference and protection by police, so serious that its investigation was made the subject of a separate part of the final report.

Chapter 14

"Scum Downs", "Letters of Comfort"

The first area of investigation concerned what was termed Process Corruption which in one of its many forms, consists of breaking the rules in order to obtain a conviction that might otherwise not have been possible for lack of evidence. If one casts one's mind back to the aide system practised in London, where embryo CID officers were trained into the art of "noble cause" perjury, then there is a ready-made example of what was found in NSW. The first and most obvious reason for this kind of dishonesty is, of course, a genuine belief in the guilt of the defendant, coupled with pressure from above to get results. Consciences may be satisfied by that certainty of guilt and the underlying immorality involved is then easily brushed aside. Other illegal means of obtaining a conviction can include interference with identification processes, bullying suspects into confessing, and by means of whatever other threats a fertile mind can devise. Legislation similar to the Police and Criminal Evidence Act 1984, regulating police behaviour in the UK, was under consideration during the mid-1990s in NSW as its provisions have been shown to be very effective in curbing police misconduct. Under that statute, all aspects of a prisoner's detention are recorded by a designated custody sergeant acting independently of those responsible for arrest and evidence gathering. The application of some 16 years' experience of working within the bounds of that statute has resulted in relatively few successful challenges to the lawfulness or fairness of anything done to a defendant in custody, after being given careful consideration by the appellate courts.

The Royal Commission's report reviews a number of instances where illegal methods were used to secure convictions, referring to one practice known among officers as a "scrum down" in which officers who were to give dishonest testimony in a case would meet to compare their evidence and tidy up loose ends and errors. So heavy was the editing and tidying up that one officer told the Commission that he was required to give evidence of events at which he was not present, from a statement written by another officer on his behalf. He admitted that he had learned from others how to manipulate evidence in the same way that an apprentice learns his trade, by following examples and then practising what he has seen. In another instance, the Commission interviewed three officers who each admitted that, whilst assisting the Major Crime Squad, they lied on oath about aspects of a search of premises, signed statements prepared for them by others and conspired with them to present their perjured evidence at court.

Nor was it only Detectives who were prepared to lie, because the Commission uncovered a serious conspiracy to defeat the ends of justice by a group of uniformed officers, anxious to ensure a conviction of a drugs dealer. Three of them, led by their Sergeant, went to a restaurant in the Kings' Cross area to make an under-cover purchase of drugs, but something went wrong and one of them, a woman officer, was assaulted. A plot was then hatched to bring the restaurant proprietor before a court for breaches of his licence terms as a "payback" for the assault. To assist in the prosecution, another officer was brought in who agreed to make a false statement in corroboration of the officer who had been earlier assaulted. In order to do this he was obliged to destroy his official notebook containing an accurate record of the event and to rewrite it to agree with his false evidence. The prosecution against the restaurateur failed when the magistrate hearing the charges became suspicious and made it plain that he believed the police evidence to be false.

Matters did not rest there, however, because on the same evening as the assault, the woman officer and another of the group came upon the suspected drugs dealer who was promptly arrested for possession of drugs. The male officer confessed to the Commission that he had planted drugs on the suspect from a supply hoarded after a previous unconnected drugs operation, leaving other officers to search him and find the "evidence". The dealer was convicted and sentenced to imprisonment but, after the truth had been revealed to the Commission, that unjust conviction was overturned. The Commission expressed disappointment that the dishonest officers had drawn others into their conspiracy, opening up to a risk of involvement, those unsuspecting officers who had searched the suspect without knowing the true source of the drugs they found on him.

The Commission expressed a view that conduct such as had been described in these cases was motivated by pressure to keep up acceptable conviction rates; that a culture of perjury had almost reached an art form among some officers, and they firmly held belief that there was a great difference between manipulating evidence to convict wrongdoers and corrupt conduct for personal gain.

Another aspect of this form of corruption is when an

investigation is deliberately undermined at either the investigation stage or when preparing the case papers for court, with the intention of wrecking the chances of a successful prosecution. There can be many motives for wishing to sabotage a prosecution including the protection of a relative, friend or colleague, but more reprehensible is when the motive is one of being paid for doing so, such as has been seen in the course of reviewing London's Porn Squad trials. The Commission suggested a number of reasons why officers had compromised investigations including bribery; the desire to cultivate informers; improper friendships with criminals; or as recompense for theft by the police, of money or goods seized from offenders who might otherwise complain.

The methods by which these objects could be attained were many and various. One often sees a tendency in cases brought by British officers to charge defendants with the most serious offences which, at first sight, seem appropriate but are reduced to a sustainable level at the instance of prosecuting counsel or trial Judge. For example, assault with intent to commit grievous bodily harm carries a maximum penalty of life imprisonment, whereas the same crime with comparably serious injury but without the necessary intent carries a maximum of five years. Whilst it is not easy to stretch facts to encompass the more serious offence where it is based heavily upon physical evidence, to tailor them in such a way as to make the lesser charge more appropriate is much simpler when carefully tailored verbal evidence is agreeable to a defendant. In drugs' cases there is a substantial difference in sentencing between one who possesses drugs for personal use and the offender who has them with intention to supply another. Here, of course, it is possible by manipulating confession evidence to incriminate a defendant in the more serious charge, instances of which the Commission often discovered. However, if there is a strong enough incentive, then the downgrading of evidence to support only the lesser crime is simplicity itself in the hands of a dishonest and greedy officer.

Almost the first thought entering the mind of a person who has been arrested and charged is to get out of custody and on bail if at all possible. It is only in a relatively small proportion of cases where objections to bail are raised by the police, generally on the grounds of the defendant's likelihood of absconding, with consideration being given to the seriousness of the crime and the probability of imprisonment. A previous record of absconding from bail and previous convictions will have an impact on the decision to grant bail or remand in custody. The natural anxiety for freedom on bail provides a fruitful source of profit to the dishonest officer because an application for bail generally comes in the early stage of proceedings before the prosecution case has been fully prepared. When an officer makes no more than a half-hearted objection to bail, omits to mention the applicant's previous convictions, or does not draw attention to earlier breaches of bail, the chances of a court granting bail are much improved. Payment to NSW officers for such favours was common, often with very large sums of money changing hands.

In many cases investigated by the Commission, there was an element of influence shown in the outcome of prosecutions by apparent carelessness or incompetence.

Evidence was sometimes"lost" and potentially valuable witnesses could not be traced. Cleverly crafted loopholes were left in case papers, through which experienced defence lawyers could find a path to acquittal of their clients and, if all else failed, there was always a "letter of comfort" to help keep a sentence to a lower level than it might otherwise have been.

A letter of comfort is a legitimate device for rewarding a person at the point of sentence for some valuable assistance to police and therefore to society. A similar system operates in the UK courts but is known colloquially as providing a "brown envelope" to the Judge who is to pass sentence. The envelope will contain a report by an officer involved in the case, setting out precise details of help which the defendant has given that is considered worthy of a reduction of the impending sentence. The report, which must have been certified as accurate by a senior officer, is seen by defence counsel and his client before being passed to the sentencing Judge by the prosecutor. It is rare for existence of the report or its contents to be referred to in open court because reports of this nature will frequently name other offenders, so that revealing its content might well prove dangerous to the defendant. It would be a naive officer who could say there is no room for corruption in connection with these letters, or that the assistance they claim is always genuine and not motivated for some corrupt purpose.

The Commission's final report details some case studies, in particular Operation Hawkesbury, as examples of what was discovered in the course of its inquiry, and the first of these concerns events in the Kings Cross district of Sydney, a place having many of the characteristics of London's Soho. At various times a centre for prostitution, brothels, illegal gambling and the haunt of major criminals. Policing such areas can be hazardous from the point of view of physical danger and by reason of temptations thrust in front of officers who are obliged to deal with its problems. Where a substantial element with commercial interests in keeping the police off their backs gather to ply their particular trades, there will inevitably be corruption. One of the many policemen who, whilst working from Kings Cross police station, fell into the trap was Detective Larry Churchill who had become involved in a conspiracy with local criminals to supply Class B drugs and to collect protection money from others. When Churchill went on holiday, he recruited another officer to look after these activities in his absence, but his choice of a co-conspirator was poor because that officer reported the matter to the Internal Police Security Unit (IPSU). The unit carried out investigations into Churchill's activities and, although it eventually managed to bring Churchill before a court where he pleaded guilty to a conspiracy to supply amphetamines, its efforts were regarded by the Commission as being, at best, superficial and inept. Later, when more effective inquiries were made by the Commission's investigators and the whole story became known, Commissioner Wood described the IPSU's investigation as a missed opportunity to address corruption in the patrol.

In court it was accepted that Churchill and another Detective agreed to reduce charges against an arrested drugs dealer and promised that they would protect him in any other drugs activities he might undertake at a cost to him of $A10,000. A further $A10,000 was demanded of a man named Colin Fisk as payment for bail to be arranged for one of his criminal associates, and on his return from holiday Churchill and Fisk met to divide the profits from their drugs sales and settle their outstanding accounts. The IPSU investigators intercepted a telephone call from Detective Sergeant Kim Thompson to Churchill, warning him that there was "a whale in the bay", a colloquialism for there being internal investigators in the area taking an interest in the Kings Cross Detectives. Unfortunately for Thompson this intercepted call by the IPSU was used to make him subject to disciplinary proceedings. At the disciplinary hearing he admitted having telephoned Churchill to warn him of impending trouble, but insisted that he did not know the substance of the complaint against Churchill, assuming it to be concerned only with his competence and performance as a Detective.

The Churchill affair came before the Police Tribunal who called Senior Detective Sergeant Fowler, the Kings Cross Chief of Detectives as a witness. He admitted having been to lunch with Churchill and a "businessman" named Wang, who was at that time subject to investigation by another police unit. He also agreed that he had been on holiday with Churchill and Wang to the Phillippines at the businessman's expense, and even more reprehensibly, admitted falsifying his official notebook to show himself on duty in Sydney during that absence from the country. And yet, regardless of these instances of blatant indiscretion and falsity, the Tribunal found him not guilty of a number of disciplinary matters. The eventual outcome of this incident and that of Thompson's own efforts to frustrate the IPSU's inquiry, was that although they had both survived unscathed, they were transferred to other stations for a time, but later at their own request were posted back to the Kings Cross detective office in their supervisory ranks.

What soon became obvious to the Commission in looking into this and other affairs was that internal investigatory units leaked information to such an alarming extent that suspected officers were usually tipped off in time to get their stories ready. They saw the culture of silence, the closing of ranks, and the activities of officers "running interference" to protect their mates, however dishonest they might be, operating at full flood.

Trevor Haken joined the police service at the age of 19, and completed basic training before his first posting to active duty. As he was to tell the Commission, he soon became drawn into minor corruption, being schooled by his seniors in ways of supplementing his salary. He learned of spotting fees, i.e., commissions paid by tow-truck operators and undertakers, to officers who dealt with road traffic accidents needing break-down facilities, or cases of sudden death in which a body had to be removed to hospital or mortuary. Such a system was not peculiar to Australia because in the 1970s, when motorways were spreading across Britain, some firms who operated heavy break-down vehicles were delighted to pay officers a modest fee for priority in getting first call to an accident. In an office close to the M1, a group of traffic police officers were found to have been milking the system until covert cameras, installed in the office ceiling, caught them at it. Greed seems to have got the better of discretion and when a motorist who could and would have arranged his own vehicle removal found it whipped away, almost from under his nose thus putting him to unnecessary expense, he registered a bitter complaint which led to the investigation. After this embarrassing incident, a formal call-out system was put in place of the cosy and lucrative *ad hoc* arrangement, so that an officer needing such help at the scene was obliged to pass the request to his controller who would then select the next operator on an approved list.

Haken went on to Chatswood station as a junior Detective and soon found himself in a web of corruption involving drugs and the criminals who traded in them. He found, too, that it was a Detective's duty to "hold the line" in the event of trouble by learning his part in whatever story had been agreed, and sticking to that story in the face of investigation. In a period of three years with an anti-drug trafficking unit he became aware of and indeed, involved in, the whole range of corrupt behaviour which the drugs trade spawns. In his unit there were occasional meetings of the "Christmas club", a group of officers actively involved in theft from drugs dealers of both money, and drugs which were re-sold, as well as in taking bribes and protection payments. At the "Christmas party" a function not confined to December but held periodically throughout the year, money collected from these sources was distributed among its members. However, there came a time when disputes arose claiming an unfair division of the money; with that and other unrelated complaints about him, Haken, whose unofficial job it was to organise the payout, was transferred to another station.

In due time, he was transferred to the King Cross detective office where he was met by two Sergeants, who drew him into the local version of the "Christmas club", this time known as "the laugh". Sergeants Thompson and Fowler, on their return to duty at Kings Cross quickly teamed up with Haken as a kindred spirit. Within a short time of this new liaison at Kings Cross, Haken found that what had begun years before as a haphazard arrangement between Detectives and criminals to capitalise on the drugs trade, had developed into a well organised network of dealers who could operate with impunity, knowing that there would be little police interference. By this time, Haken had been recognised as a man with a serious drink problem which, together with suspicions about his other activities, brought him to the notice of the Internal Affairs branch who carried out an investigation which resulted in his being summoned before the NSW Crime Commission (NSWCC), where he denied any wrongdoing. It seems that, in many instances, suspected officers had only to deny involvement in criminal activities for those assertions to be accepted without serious challenge and such was the case here.

Haken did not "roll over" as a matter of conscience because, although he had been able to satisfy the NSWCC at the previous appearance, his next brush with authority was rather more difficult when he was ordered to appear before the Royal Commission. Its interrogators were of a more dogged character and, moreover, had carried out extensive electronic surveillance of his activities. Faced with the inevitable, he decided to co-operate and in a very short time, revealed himself as a prize beyond value. Not only did his co-operation and a mass of specific information result in a major break through for the Commission in its pursuit of corruption in many of its forms but, quite incidentally, gave it an insight into how corruption infiltrated the service to infect otherwise honest young juniors. The Commission learned about examples of corrupt practices, of which they had no previous knowledge and the identity of officers involved in all manner of dishonest practices who had, until then, been beyond suspicion.

Haken agreed to work undercover for the Commission and did so for almost a year providing even more information and evidence to form the core of its final success. One of his efforts concerned his old colleague Fowler, now promoted to Inspector. Seated in a car in which a tiny camera had been installed, the Inspector was pictured accepting money from Haken in circumstances which could only be interpreted as dishonest. Fowler was ordered to attend before the Commission but declined, claiming that he had been injured and was unwell. Unhappily for him, he had told Haken of his intention to claim injury as a reason for non-attendance before the accident had actually happened. This intended deception, too, was recorded by the industrious Mr Haken and a threat of arrest brought Fowler before Commissioner Wood, where he refused to answer any questions, but suggested that an actor had been hired to double for him in order to produce fabricated evidence. In due course he was dismissed the service but escaped prosecution.

Haken's undercover work for the Commission was especially valuable in cracking the "code of silence": that protective screen that officers drew around themselves as a means of insulating their activities against the outside world. It was told how officers, once it was known that an investigation was under way and that someone had "rolled over", met to discuss the front that they should put up if called upon to give evidence. Despite these measures, a number of them gave up what was becoming recognised as an impossible means of avoiding detection, and admitted their part in various instances of corrupt conduct. Among them were Detective Sergeants Kim Thompson, Neville Scullion, John Swan and Detective Constable Duncan Demol. Scullion, in a recorded conversation with Haken, was heard to explain how he would forestall a complaint he was ordered to investigate, made against a brother officer of having robbed and beaten a suspect. In essence, it would be to put difficulties in the complainant's way in the hope that he would become disillusioned with the matter and let it drop. All were eventually dismissed the service without facing criminal charges.

Haken's reward was an indemnity against prosecution although his time in the police service was at an end and he was granted access to the full witness protection scheme. He was not called to give evidence and many questions were raised as to why a man as active as he in corruption should not have been put into the witness box to testify against other officers in criminal proceedings. In the course of an interview with the press, Mr Nicholas Cowdrey, QC, the Director of Public Prosecutions, pointed out that Haken's credibility would have been severely challenged by the defence. One can see all manner of suggestions being put to him on behalf of one or more defendants, most potent being that his evidence was being tailored to reduce his own punishment, rather than to establish the truth. There is always a risk in calling an accomplice, such as Haken, and sensible prosecutors avoid doing so if there is other more reliable evidence. Many cases have been thrown away for just such a misjudgment of tactics and there are other ways in which a corrupt officer's services can be dispensed with.

The proliferation of possible criminal charges involving police officers in the wake of the Commission's report was such that the DPP complained of a lack of additional funding and a shortage of courts and court time needed to deal with them. There were inevitable delays in bringing cases before the courts, but cases did not always simply go away. This was very true in the case of six officers who are alleged to have been involved in beating up prisoners at Kings Cross station, and their subsequent perversion of the course of justice. Swan was one of those suspected of being concerned, as was a Sergeant who had been a prosecuting officer for many years. The wheels of bureaucracy are often as slow as those of justice; however, all six were brought before a court at the beginning of May 2000, charged with a variety of offences of assault and perversion of justice.

Chapter 15

Operation Post - The Stabbing that did not Happen

In December 1984, the Australian Commonwealth and Joint Task Force (JTF), had been engaged in a long-term investigation, code named *Operation Post*, set up with the aim of arresting and convicting a major drugs dealer. Ready to spring a trap, they had him penned up in a lane but in a desperate attempt to escape, he tried to climb over a corrugated iron fence. He was pulled down and arrested but in the scuffle, one of the officers received an unpleasant arm wound for which he later received a payment as victim's compensation. The police report into his arrest claimed that the defendant had made verbal admissions to stabbing the officer in his failed escape attempt. The truth of this admission was supported to a large extent by the subsequent finding of a bloodstained knife at the scene. At court, the defendant entered a plea of guilty to a less serious offence than that with which he was first charged and received a commensurately lower sentence of imprisonment. Looking at this narrative one would be entitled to regard the case as unexceptional with no taint of injustice surrounding it. The reality however, was quite different.

The matter came before the Commission for investigation in the wake of Haken's revelations and in the climate of discomfort, apprehension, fear, troubled consciences or however else one might describe the state of mind of those with something to hide, information about the true scenario flooded into the Commission's offices, soon to be converted into hard evidence. In reality, almost the entire case against the defendant had been based on perjury, planting of evidence and a disgraceful example of forced plea bargaining.

Whilst it was true that the defendant had been arrested in the lane, the rest of the story was false, even to his plea of guilty, which was entered, as he explained, because he had spent time in custody for which he would receive a substantial discount, but an equally pressing motive was that he had no wish to bring down the wrath of the JTF in the future by making allegations against its officers which had no chance of being believed. In 1995, in a bizarre reversal of roles, his denial of the stabbing to the Commission was corroborated by police who had been in the lane at the time of his arrest and had later made statements describing the non-existent stabbing. Before the Commission, three of them stated that they had not seen their colleague stabbed as they had claimed some nine years earlier and could not, therefore, corroborate his story of the attack.

Shortly after his arrest, the script for his "admissions" to the stabbing was agreed among the team with the dual purpose of charging the defendant with causing harm and to provide a more dramatic reason for the officer's injury, rather than an accident while trying to climb the iron fence. Another officer, by now having been promoted to a senior rank, admitted to the Commission that it was he who had, on instructions, taken a knife smeared with the "victim's" blood to the scene where it could be found by other officers and made an exhibit in the case. This incident was brought to light by Haken who was present at the police station immediately after the arrest, and was able to give the Commission the whole story, including the agreement to "salt" the scene with a bloodstained knife.

***

In 1983, Haken and other officers were engaged in investigating an incident in which shots had been fired at the home of a Mr Bayeh, in what was believed to be some kind of turf war between two rival criminal factions in the Kings Cross area. Soon afterwards, Haken and his colleague were given the names of two suspects who were duly arrested on behalf of Detectives in charge of that investigation. Interests involved in the affair paid the two officers a large sum of money to ensure that they did not "verbal" the suspects when recording the events surrounding the arrests, and also to use their knowledge of police procedures to help them to frustrate the continuing investigation. Before formal interviews between the suspects and the officers in the case could take place, Haken advised them how to put a story together which would make their conviction less certain. It may seem an odd form of blackmail for police to agree not to concoct false evidence in return for cash, but it must be appreciated how powerful verbal admissions were when guilt or innocence was being determined in court. The technique is not unknown, and was part of the evidence against the "Coathanger" officers, who blackmailed Perry as described in Chapter 4. Major reforms in the UK contained in the Police and Criminal Evidence Act 1984, more or less cured any propensity for officers to continue the time honoured practice of "verballing", but it was still going strong in Australia for some time to come. The Bayeh incident was far from being the only such example of this form of corruption because illegally extracting money from suspects and defendants was a common area of investigation by the Commission.

***

Skimming off a proportion of cash and drugs found in the course of raids and investigations was a regular feature of many drugs arrests, but because the offender was reluctant to attract any further attention from the police, such thefts were only rarely reported to higher authority. In "Operation Pickup", eight members of the JTF succeeded in arresting two major drugs offenders in possession of cannabis resin and more than A$40,000 in cash, which was probably the pay-off from a drugs' sale they had been seen to make earlier.

In a car they had been using the police found A$6,000 and a search of a garage known to be used by them revealed cocaine, drugs paraphernalia and about A$200,000 in cash. The A$40,000 found on them was taken to the station and recorded in proper form but the officers who searched the car later managed to steal some of the A$6,000. The largest amount, which had been found in the garage was eventually shared out among some of the JTF members including those who had not even been present during this particular operation.

There was a measure of dissatisfaction with the way in which this large sum was apportioned between them and it was this, together with other matters that lead to Haken's transfer from the team.

Haken, in his evidence to the Commission, explained that something had gone badly wrong with regard to the money booked in because some of the cash from the car was found to be missing, but only after science branch personnel, unknown to the officers who searched it, had photographed the money showing serial numbers of the notes. There were other officers involved in this operation apart from Haken and the hard core of dishonest members, and he realised there was a danger of the theft blowing up in their faces. He had, with some difficulty, managed to recover the stolen notes and return them to their proper place. His efforts to repair the situation were successful, because although it had happened in 1983, it was not until his revelations to the Commission that the truth emerged.

***

There were many officers who gave evidence to the Commission of having received money from gambling operators, by means of blackmail and protection payments or as a reward for giving them information about impending police raids. Haken himself told of payments he had received from Chinatown gambling establishments as protection money which he shared with colleagues, even though the control and suppression of gambling was no part of his job and he could not, therefore, give anything of value in return. Detective Senior Constable Deborah Locke, of whom more will be heard later, told the Commission that there was a high proportion of raids where it was obvious that the officers were expected, reinforcing the evidence of selected operators being protected from police action by the very people who were supposed to be upholding the law. It was known before the Commission began its investigations that there were many unhealthy associations between Gaming Squad officers and gaming interests, one example of which was a squad member's close friendship with a man he knew to be a supplier of illegal gaming machines. Not only did the supplier attend the officer's wedding as a valued friend, but he also provided the police cricket team with a set of shirts.

***

In the early hours of a morning in June 1992, at French's Forest police station, North Sydney, a young Constable, Andrew Bourke, was shot by a masked man who had entered the station through a side door. The man had a sawn off shotgun and fired it at the officer, hitting him in the shoulder just as he was reaching for his personal weapon. Only by good fortune did the injury not prove fatal and after some months he was able to go back to his job. The investigating officers at the time said that his attacker had entered the station and demanded to be given firearms but, after shooting the constable, was chased by him along the road for a 100 yards or so until he collapsed from pain and weakness. The gunman was never traced.

Detective Inspector Mike Hagen of the North Region Homicide Squad was put in initial charge of the investigation and it eventually became the responsibility of the North Region Major Crime Squad. During their inquiries they learned of a suspicion that the shooting was connected to an alleged involvement of police officers in the distribution of marijuana. Once this suspicion had been brought to light, the possibility of police involvement in a criminal activity should, by law, have been referred at once to the Police Ombudsman and the ICAC. Officers attached to the Internal Affairs Branch (IAB) engaged on reviewing the progress of the investigation into the shooting knew quite well what was being alleged about police involvement, but chose not to inform either of the two relevant authorities. When *The Sydney Morning Herald* unearthed the allegations eight months later and informed the Ombudsman, he demanded a report from the Commissioner of Police. This was only one of many instances where the proper notification had not been made: it was only a month earlier that Mr Landa, the Ombudsman, had criticised the police for failing to report an attempt at suicide by a young man in their custody.

By this time, the activities of the IAB itself had become a target for bitter criticism from all sides with a vested interest in maintaining the *status quo.* Understandably perhaps, rank and file officers looked upon them as enemies to whom nothing should be voluntarily revealed, whilst in contrast at higher levels in both police service and political circles its members' integrity and efficiency were becoming suspect. So serious was the view taken by Mr Griffiths, Minister for Police, that he instructed the Inspector General of Police to review the role of the Professional Responsibilities office whose head, Assistant Commissioner Cole, had overall responsibility for the activities of the IAB. In addition, he arranged a meeting of the State Crime Commission to consider terms of reference for a review of the police internal investigation in which there had been an apparent failure to follow the matter through. Interviewed by the press, Mr Griffiths, when asked on February 25 if he thought that "heads would roll", is quoted as saying, "I certainly do, but I will not pre-empt whose, because I believe that allegations have to be fully investigated first". On the following Monday, Assistant Commissioner Cole reported sick, seeking treatment for stress. He did not return to duty, having been certified as permanently unfit.

Regardless of the truth of allegations of police involvement leading to Constable Bourke's wounding, an examination of the part taken by the IAB shows either that it had followed a pattern of total disregard of its duty of reporting a clearly defined range of matters, or alternatively it was lending its hand to an orchestrated cover-up. In the knowledge that allegations of corruption against officers must be reported for independent consideration, it is difficult to believe that the IAC was so inefficient or so naive.

A matter even more serious had arisen in June 1981, when Detective Sergeant Roger Rogerson shot and killed a man named Warren Lanfranchi, a known drugs dealer, in Chippendale. At the Coroner's inquest the jury declined to bring in a verdict that Lanfranchi was killed in lawful self-defence but the Coroner, nevertheless, made a finding that Lanfranchi had died from a gunshot wound to the chest, inflicted on him by the officer whilst endeavouring to make an arrest. The effect of this decision was to clear Rogerson of blame for the man's untimely end.

Some three years later, Detective Sergeant Mick Drury

of the Drugs Squad was shot and injured at his home.

A task force was set up by Superintendent McDonald but after considerable efforts, no charges could be brought and the matter was regarded as inconclusive. In the course of the task force inquiries, however, a number of allegations about police involvement in drugs offences were made, together with suggestions of protection money being sought; bribery and witnesses being encouraged to commit perjury. Although the main object of the task force's job had not been satisfactorily concluded, at the instance of the Crown Advocate, Rogerson was charged with an offence of attempting to bribe Sergeant Drury into changing his evidence in an impending drugs trial. When Rogerson's case came for trial before a jury in 1985, Rogerson was acquitted. It was not the end of the matter, however, because within a matter of weeks, departmental charges (disciplinary charges) were brought against him for improperly associating with known criminals and impairing the efficiency of the service.

In May 1985, Rogerson, under surveillance at Kingsford Smith airport (otherwise known as Mascot), was seen to meet a young woman to whom he handed a bag which was found to contain packets of white powder. In exchange he received a holdall containing a large amount of money in $50 notes. The lady, using the pseudonym "Miss Jones" was a drug addict and she gave evidence at Rogerson's subsequent trial that they had indeed changed bags at the airport in the way described. In that same month, he and a man named Maurice Nowytarger opened two bank accounts with the National Australia bank in false names and deposited A$110,000. Naturally enough, the circumstances aroused further interest in the investigating officers who, taking all the circumstances into account, were certain that Rogerson and his associate were engaged in some form of crime.

On July 1, Rogerson and Nowytarger were seen on the bank's close circuit security cameras where they had gone to close the accounts. On July 11 or 12, a police officer leaked the information to Rogerson that he had been photographed with a known criminal, a piece of intelligence that set alarm bells ringing in his mind. Within days he had begun a process intended to show that the money had been acquired legitimately and to that end he and Nowytarger met in a restaurant with Dr Nicholas Paltos and a solicitor named Ross Karp. The group came to an agreement that documents would be prepared to show how some of the money had got into the suspect accounts, the basis of which would be the purported sale of a Bentley car to Karp for A$60,000 with the sale agreement backdated to December 1983, with Nowytarger described as the vendor.

On July 24, Rogerson phoned a Detective Inspector Strong, saying that he had heard there were police officers who would like to be able to prove that the money he had withdrawn from the bank was the result of crime. His object in calling was to offer the earliest possible explanation for his possession of the money. At his trial for conspiracy to pervert the course of justice, he maintained that the Bentley sale was genuine and that he had been accumulating stage payments from Karp, in a biscuit tin, since 1983. Almost the whole purchase price was in his possession by November 1984, but Karp did not see the car until July 1985, when the backdated contract of sale had been signed. He explained to the jury that the long delay between agreement and final purchase was due to his having done a lot of work on the car in the interim. Rogerson, Paltos and Nowytarger were convicted and appealed to the New South Wales Court of Appeal. The grounds of appeal were, broadly, that the prosecution had not identified a specific crime; therefore there could not be a conspiracy to pervert the course of justice. The appellate court upheld their appeal and quashed their convictions. The prosecution then took the unusual step of asking the High Court of Australia to overturn that decision and were successful in the cases of Rogerson and Paltos. The court ordered that the Court of Appeal of New South Wales's judgment be set aside and the matter remitted to it for determination in accordance with the superior court's judgment. The final result was that Rogerson and Paltos's convictions were reinstated.

Rogerson was dismissed from the service in 1986, but there was a further trial in which he was charged with conspiracy to murder Sergeant Drury; however he was once again acquitted.

Chapter 16

Informants, Informers and Whistleblowers

Informants, informers and whistleblowers are all terms denoting the giving of information but each has its own connotations, good or bad, when applied to crime and police activities. A generalisation but nevertheless useful, is that an informant is one who tells of what has happened or may be going to happen in the future. His or her information may be about ordinary mundane matters or facts of great importance but does not necessarily require any motives of ill-will in passing it on. The word informer, however, has become a pejorative one from which such words as "grass", "copper's nark", "rat", "snout", "dog" and, in Ireland, "tout" have been derived. In Australia, the phrase to "dob in" can be used to describe the action of informer, informant or whistleblower depending upon its context and the motives of the "dobber". Whistleblowers are generally regarded as those closely associated with someone who is misusing their power or responsibilities, and who attempt to get authority to do something about it. Later in this chapter we shall look at some instances of whistleblowers in the police environment, but to illustrate an extreme example of actions which have been directed against an individual, the medical profession takes some beating.

Professor Stephen Bolsin, an anaesthetist, is a case in point. Employed in the paediatric unit at Bristol Royal Infirmary, he soon became concerned about the high mortality rate among babies who underwent heart surgery and came to the conclusion that two of the surgeons performing the operations lacked the necessary skills for such delicate work. He first drew the attention of the hospital's medical administrator to the problem but having received a rebuff, took the matter to the General Medical Council. The outcome, after a comprehensive hearing, was to strike the most senior surgeon, and the medical administrator off the register, and to ban the other surgeon from operating on small children for a period.

One might have expected approval from the profession for what he had achieved in rectifying a tragic situation where lives were at risk, but the reverse was the case. Villified and ostracised in the most cruel way, with every application for posts being blocked over a long period, he and his family moved to Australia in order to rebuild his professional life. Even there he was pursued for breaking the code of silence, when a doctor telephoned the hospital where was working, telling the administration that "... he was the most hated anaesthetist in Europe". If highly intelligent and educated people whose professional duty is to put patients' welfare before any other consideration can throw a self-interested shield around wayward colleagues, what can one hope for from lesser mortals?

The Public Interest Disclosure Act 1998 was passed in an effort to protect those who disclose information which they believe it to be the right thing to do. The concept of *protected disclosure* is contained in the legislation which means, in effect, that subject to certain provisos the informant is shielded from dismissal for having revealed the information. A short summary of sections 1 and 2 will be found in Appendix 2, but, as with all summaries, only a study of the full text should be made by those who wish to know more.

As this study of corruption has shown from so many

sources, informers can often be the central figures to much police misuse of power for which the only protection is a rigid control of their employment. Effective supervision and control has not yet been achieved in many instances, as the following recent press reports show.

A Detective Constable in the Flying Squad was caught stealing by an anti-corruption team and, either because of a crisis of conscience or a hope of a degree of mercy, informed on a number of his colleagues. He was sentenced to nine years' imprisonment and had by then already spent many months on remand in protective custody. The prison authorities will be hard put to it to continue that protection because he will be regarded by most inmates as not only a hated ex-policeman, but also as an informer on whom their personal frustrations can find a violent outlet.

The Royal Commission has relied heavily upon those who reported misconduct and corruption in the early stages of its work, when those who gave the information were referred to as internal informers with that expression's unfortunate connotations. This was changed to "internal witnesses" in an attempt to make the practice less unattractive among staff and a programme was set up to offer them protection from victimisation. A few examples of how such people have fared will demonstrate the need for a firm and, as far as can be, effective regimen of protection both physically and socially.

It may be recalled that in the London Metropolitan Police porn trial of November 1976, Detective Inspector Anthony Kilkeer gave exceedingly damaging evidence against a group of officers including Chief Inspector Charles

Fenwick, to the effect that he had tried to involve him in the team's criminal activities. At first reading of his evidence, the story of having thrown away the first money given to him may have sounded implausible, then to allow further sums to build up in his unlocked office drawer hoping that it would simply go way, even more so. However, after a gruelling three days of examination and cross-examination in court, his evidence must have retained a ring of truth because it was accepted by the jury. Shortly after the trial he was heard to remark that he did not contemplate a future in the police service, realising that he would be regarded as being no longer a team player.

Very similar evidence was given to the Commission by a young detective within the Haken sphere of influence in NSW who, so disturbed by being given money in a share out, tore it up on the first occasion and afterwards let the money accumulate in his desk drawer. That he and Kilkeer, two officers half a world away and separated from each other by 20 years in time, resorted to these actions, speaks volumes about the mental stress that can be suffered by honest men obliged to serve with dishonest colleagues.

The case of Deborah Locke, a Sydney officer, is another illustration of the abominable way internal witnesses can be treated unless given the protection supposedly built into the system. She was a Senior Detective Constable with 10 years of admirable service behind her when, in 1994, Mr Hatton forced the Government into setting up the Royal Commission. During the debate he drew attention to instances of unjust treatment to a number of internal witnesses within the service, of which one was Deborah Locke. As she revealed to *The Sydney Morning Herald* next day, she had been subjected to disgraceful sexual discrimination, the worst of which came when she applied for maternity leave. "They told me maternity leave was prostitution, I was being paid for being on my back and getting pregnant. I was told to resign and I was a burden and they would have to carry me". Of more direct concern for present purposes was the treatment meted out to her as a purported "whistleblower". So serious were the effects on her health that acute stress, which was likely to have brought on pneumonia and meningitis, was also blamed by her for the miscarriage of her baby. The Premier, in the course of the debate made a full public apology to her and a brother officer, Mr Kimbal Cook, for the "shabby treatment" to which they had been subjected.

Cook was a Detective Sergeant with the Gaming Squad, as was Deborah Locke, when they were engaged in an operation leading to the arrest of a leading SP (starting price) bookmaker. In 1993 Cook had informed on two officers, Detectives Deek and Zubrecki to the ICAC and as a result they were subsequently jailed for having entered into a corrupt relationship with the bookmaker. As so often happens, his revelation and its aftermath put him beyond the pale in the self-protecting police community, and serious harassment from his colleagues in the squad began. Cook became so concerned for his own and his family's physical safety that he was obliged to spend money on security arrangements but instead of simply accepting this enforced expense, he applied to the service for reimbursement of the costs. One can imagine the consternation that an application of this kind would have made upon the official mind, increased no doubt by a request from the ICAC for details of the policy and guidelines concerning the subject matter which had led to his request for payment.

As part of the service's response, Assistant Commissioner J. Jarrett called for a draft policy on "whistle-blowers" to be drawn up and in late 1994, a firm of outside consultants was commissioned to review the existing policies and make recommendations for improvement.

Unhappily for Deborah Locke she was suspected, quite wrongly, to be part of the "dobbing in" of the two Detectives and became a target for all the unpleasantness her colleagues were capable of heaping upon her. Although she was transferred to a different station, there was no escape and she found herself branded as a troublemaker with the harassment continuing unabated. Whilst she herself had been caught up in the backlash against Cook, it was now the turn of her husband, a Fraud Squad Detective to be cold-shouldered by other members of the service as though he had, by association, some responsibility for Deek and Zubrecki's convictions. The fact that other officers who had supported Locke were subjected to various forms of harassment as well, is a graphic illustration of the self-protection mechanism in action, in which honest officers can be torn between their moral inclinations and loyalty to even those comrades they know to be dishonest.

Locke later gave evidence to the Commission about the activities of the Gaming Squad, in particular their friendship and drinking habits with wholly unsuitable people. She described long alcohol filled lunches with well-known criminals at their expense, and of numerous occasions when as part of the team raiding premises it was quite obvious to her that the operators had been tipped off in advance. She spoke of the debilitating effect of the silent disapproval of her colleagues saying, "It's an ongoing thing. Continually going into the Police Credit Union is a stressful situation for me. I don't know who I'm going to run into. People hear rumours. I'm seen as a dog, someone who has spoken out, and it's not what you do with the culture in the police force".

Locke had, some years earlier, revealed that an Inspector was in improper relationship with criminals and, following his dismissal, was forming improper relationships with serving police officers. In 1994, she drew attention to irregularities in the Fraud Squad including alleged abuses of travel allowance claims. There was swift retaliation, traced back to the dismissed Inspector's continuing influence and she was subjected to investigation over an allegedly false travel expense claim she had made some four years earlier. There was no doubt but that this was a "payback" or revenge complaint which was not resolved in her favour for an incredible delay of 18 months. The incident and its delay convinced Ms Locke that there was no future for her in the service and she was granted a medical discharge.

Leaving New South Wales and turning to Wales for a moment. In the UK, *The Times* newspaper published a law report on August 24, 1999, and a brief summary of an appeal; *Regina v. Kellam, ex parte South Wales Police Authority* (see Appendix 3) shows a remarkably similar situation to that of Deborah Locke's. In essence the case established that failure on the part of the service to deal with mistreatment of those who informed against colleagues could establish grounds for action, not only for the stress caused to the informer, but also to a close relative.

In 1994, J.M. Bennet Consulting Services Pty Ltd, undertook the survey of internal witness policy on behalf of the NSW police service and at the end of their survey they reported a low level of awareness and interest in the existing policy among officers, and that too many of those who had become internal witnesses did not feel that they had been given the promised protection and anonymity. Whilst some were grateful for the attention of the appointed mentors and case officers looking into their complaint, others believed that full support from them was lacking. In March 1995, following the report from Bennet, a revision of policy was announced with the first item being a change of name from "internal informer" to "internal witness". Importantly, the definition of an internal witness was broadened from those who had volunteered information, to include those who were summoned to give evidence before the Commission, and who told of corrupt practices by former colleagues.

An Internal Witness Support Unit (IWSU) was set up and a policy of fast tracking appropriate cases was put in place to obviate a common complaint that investigations were often too slow in being resolved, thus causing unnecessary strains on complainants. Instead of mentors and case officers being appointed without reference to the complainant, sometimes with no firm knowledge of their intended function, a properly experienced case officer would be appointed and internal witnesses would be invited to nominate a senior officer in whom they had confidence to act as mentor. A mutually agreed support officer would also be appointed. The mentor would be someone to whom the witness could turn for advice, whilst the support officer would be responsible for providing support and protection within the witness's work place. Only time will tell whether or not the new arrangements will reduce instances of victimisation. However the general impression is that matters have already improved considerably. As the service gets used to the increasing current of distaste for corruption and police officers who are themselves criminals, the sooner will there be the need for fewer internal witnesses and the obligation to protect them.

The Mollen Commission's report into the NYPD (of which more later) heard evidence from officers about the code of silence, which dictates that officers do not inform on other officers. Without seeking to condone this attitude, the Commission expressed a degree of understanding:

> "This loyalty ethic itself is not corruptive. Loyalty and trust are vital attributes that promote effective and safe policing. We cannot ask police officers to abandon their loyalty to each other whilst simultaneously demanding that they confront danger for us. But group loyalty often flourishes at the expense of an officer's sworn duty. It makes allegiance to fellow officers - even corrupt ones - more important than allegiance to the Department and the community. When this happens, loyalty itself becomes corrupt and erects the strongest barriers to corruption control."

A former officer, now an admitted offender, answered questions at a public hearing in this way:

> Q. "Were you ever afraid that one of your fellow officers might turn you in?"
>
> A. "Never".
>
> Q. "Why not"?
>
> A. "Because it was the Blue Wall of Silence. Cops don't tell on cops. And if they did tell on them, say if a cop decided to tell on me, his career's ruined. He's going to be labelled as a rat. So if he's got 15 more years to go on the job, he's going to be miserable because it follows you wherever you go. And he could be in a precinct, he's going to have nobody to work with. And chances are if it comes down to it, they're going to let him get hurt."

In another case, a Detective who had served in Internal Affairs was transferred to a precinct Detective Squad. In his first week his new colleagues made sure he knew that he would be alone on the street. They placed dead rats on his car windshield, stole or destroyed his personal property, and told him directly that he could not count on them in times of danger. It is difficult to conceive of a more deadly and dispiriting attitude being adopted even by honest colleagues who could have no reason to fear his presence among them.

Regardless of what encouragement there may be to inform on corruption, be it in the medical profession, the police service or commerce and industry, whistleblowing can be a hazardous occupation, not only for the informer's peace of mind, but also his or her physical safety. It will continue to be so unless and until that wall of silence can be demolished.

Chapter 17

Royal Commission Interim Report

The Royal Commissioner issued his first interim report in February 1996 in which he concluded that the investigating framework within the service was inadequate, in need of radical reform and that there was, *prima facie,* evidence of entrenched corruption. That provisional assessment hardened in the final report to a certainty.

In January 1996, the Commissioner of Police for New South Wales, Mr Tony Lauer, tendered his resignation to take effect on February 19 of that year, 13 months earlier than his anticipated retirement date. There were no adverse references to Mr Lauer in the interim report which might have persuaded him to take that course and Mr Whelan, the Minister for Police, told a press conference that Mr Lauer was retiring because he had reached the age of 60 years [and] "... to afford the new Commissioner the opportunity to commence the reforms intended by the government ..." He also made favourable comments about Mr Lauer's work during the turbulent years during which he had served and on his efforts to rid the service of corruption. The press and Mr Hatton, the Independent MP who had sparked off the appointment of the Royal Commission, were rather less comforting. They pointed out that in spite of his insistence that there was no serious problem with corruption within the NSW police, that strongly expressed view had been refuted by a mass of evidence before the Commission. In 40 years of police service, Mr Lauer had proved himself to be a policeman's policeman, in other words one who had had personal experience of every level of the service, and the opportunity to observe all the scams and dodges of which officers were capable. It was, therefore, difficult for them to understand how barely a whiff of the rampant corruption at almost every rank ever drifted into his office and across his desk.

Mr Whelan, during the press conference, announced that appointing a new Commissioner was likely to take up to 12 months thus creating a potentially damaging hiatus and there was much speculation in the newspapers about where the new appointee would be found. The general feeling was that an internal promotion would be difficult in the light of the Commission's early findings, and there would be the demoralising effect an outside appointment would have upon those senior officers who cherished an ambition to step into Lauer's shoes. The Deputy Commissioner, Mr Neil Taylor, had announced his retirement a week before Mr Lauer's and Chief Superintendent Lysaught, Mr Lauer's chief of staff had been dismissed the service a few weeks earlier for misbehaviour which had been revealed during the Commission's investigations. To have appointed a new head from existing senior officers, even though the majority were honest and dedicated officers without the smallest taint of corruption, would have missed a momentous opportunity for a clean start to the process of reform. Mr Whelan's gloomy prediction was ill-founded because in June of that year, Mr P.J. Ryan, QPM, Msc, BA, accepted an invitation from the New South Wales Government to take up the Commissionership

Mr Ryan had begun his police service as a Constable in 1963 in the Lancashire Constabulary, rising to the rank of Superintendent before being appointed in 1983, Chief

Superintendent in the Metropolitan Police at Chelsea. By 1984 he was an Assistant Chief Constable in the North Yorkshire Police; Deputy Chief Constable of the Durham Constabulary in May 1988, and in July 1990, Chief Constable of the Norfolk Constabulary. In June 1993, he was appointed the first National Director of Police Training, a post bringing him into wide contact with police training agencies in many parts of the world, a post which resulted in his becoming the founding President of the Association of European Police Colleges.

His Fellowship of both the Institute of Management and the Institute of Personnel Management, taken together with his command experience, no doubt satisfied the NSW Governor that he was the right man for what must have been one of the most daunting tasks ever to face a career policeman. His appointment was the trigger for the most extensive of reforms ever to have been undertaken on a seriously damaged police service.

There were a number of different agencies charged with taking some part in regulating the police service, the most important of these being the Minister for Police who, by virtue of the Police Services Act 1996, s.8(1) and (5), was responsible for police policy with power to direct the Police Commissioner in matters within that area of activity. The Commissioner's responsibility lay with control and management of the service: "subject to direction by the Minister". There was no statutory definition of these individual areas with the result that Ministers and Commissioners did not always see eye-to-eye on who had the say in particular situations. The press, reporting on Mr Lauer's resignation referred to one such conflict when it said

"... he faced crisis after crisis, the most celebrated being his long-running feud with the then Minister for Police, Mr Ted Pickering, which led to the Minister's resignation ..."

Such conflicts on fundamental responsibilities in any organisation are bound to be damaging, but in a police service they have enormous potential for a disastrous breakdown in public confidence, something already lacking in New South Wales. Why there should have been such a serious breach between these two individuals does not concern us but one is entitled to reflect upon lurking dangers when one of the protagonists seeks to exercise undue political control, whilst the other tries to keep all control to himself.

In the course of the Royal Commission hearings, Justice Wood was able to identify many areas where the NSW Police problems existed with the result that in the final report, many recommendations for change could be made, of which a key recommendation was that a proper line of demarcation of responsibility between the Police Commissioner and the Police Minister should be drawn, so that any danger of political influence being applied in purely operational matters was removed, and with it a source of potential conflict.

Many of the report's recommendations are now in place, either following appropriate legislation, or by inclusion in the service's internal regulations. Of the legislation, the Police Commissioner's power to discharge officers from the service provided him with a most effective tool for the rapid disposal of those whose continuing membership was unacceptable. The Police Services Act 1990, s.181D(1), was amended by the Police Legislation Further Amendment Act, 1996, before publication of the final report, to introduce the concept of "Commissioner's Confidence", the absence of which allows the Police Commissioner to remove a police officer if he:

> "... does not have confidence in the officer's suitability to continue as a police officer, having regard to the officer's competence, integrity, performance or conduct ..."

This power cannot be exercised arbitrarily or without proper protection against someone acting in spite or by generating a false payback complaint. In the Commissioner's Confidence Protocol, it is made clear that:

> "Dedicated and committed officers have nothing to fear in relation to any alleged abuse of power under the provisions and,
>
> that each case will be considered on an individual basis with due process being observed at every stage and on every occasion and that,
>
> the Commissioner must be convinced of the reasonableness of a case before proceeding to apply the provisions."

The protocol sets out who may initiate action to bring into question the Commissioner's Confidence in an officer, including various police commands, the Police Integrity Commission (PIC), the Independent Commission Against Corruption (ICAC), the NSW Ombudsman, the NSW Crime Commission and a Royal Commissioner. It is only after an exhaustive process of investigation and consultation, notice to the subject and consideration of any submission he or she may make, that the Commissioner can exercise his power of removal. Essentially, there is no requirement that the subject must be found to have committed an offence under either internal regulation, or the criminal law, although either would have a persuasive effect in decision taking [see Appendix ... for the text of s.181].

Full and effective use is being made into the new millennium of this power. Removals under s.181 continue, and the Special Crime Unit in an operation code-named "Gymea" has resulted in over six police and 140 criminals being arrested and charged with serious crimes. This figure includes some organised crime figures previously regarded as untouchable.

Upon his taking up the new command, Mr Ryan was able to formulate new operational policies based upon many of the recommendations contained in the Commission's interim report but, rather than review those recommendations, it may be better to look at a short summary of the actual changes made. A good place to start is in parts of a paper presented by him to the Association of Chief Police Officers (ACPO) summer conference, in England in July 1999. He gave a brief review of the NSW Internal Affairs command without making any criticism of its faults before 1997 [which were many], and then proceeded to describe the situation at the time of his presentation.

"The Internal Affairs command underwent radical

structural change during the two years following the Royal Commission, incorporating a proactive investigative approach to corruption and serious misconduct involving police officers. The use of competent investigators and intelligence analysts, contemporary criminal investigative methods, physical and technological surveillance and coercive powers are now investigative standards for the command.

"The mandate to investigate not only internal matters, but external influences fostering corruption, such as organised crime, was given [by Commissioner Ryan] in 1997 ... The term, 'organised crime', often conjures up images of Al Capone and the mafia; however, in modern society, organised crime is far more sinister and aligned with corrupt police. The Internal Affairs command, adopting investigative methodologies, has begun to examine organised crime elements which are thriving in New South Wales under the protection and assistance of police.

"The term 'proactive' means to instigate measures which are designed to avoid or minimise a situation occurring, namely corruption, or prevent corruption from occurring altogether. The methods used by the Internal Affairs command are acknowledged as not being the final cure for corruption, yet serve as its prevention. (In an interview with *The Sun Herald* newspaper, Commissioner Ryan said, 'the battle against corruption was far from over ... I can never give you a corruption free police service, but I can give you a corruption resistant one'.)

"The traditional approach of targeting corrupt police

officers, however, only solves half the problem. Removing corrupt police, yet not targeting the criminals in association with those police, is not proactive. The corruption of police and government officials is simply a necessary part of doing business for the organised criminal. The influence of organised crime on corruption is therefore now a primary focus of the investigating approach of Internal Affairs.

"The Royal Commission inquiries time and again found links between the police and organised criminals. During the Kings Cross inquiries [reported by Commissioner Wood], substantial evidence was uncovered of an interdependence between police on the one hand, and drug dealers and the proprietors or managers of strip shows, brothels, nightclubs and shooting galleries on the other (ie, places where drugs users can buy an injection kit and use a room for a time in order to get a fix). Justice Wood reviewed two previous inquiries into the Kings Cross area and found compelling evidence of organised crime, yet the inquiries were unable to detect the high levels of associated corruption due to the ineffective investigative techniques used.

"The Internal Affairs command has four dedicated investigation units ... namely:

Internal Affairs Investigating Teams
Special Projects Unit
Integrity Testing Unit
Covert Unit."

Commissioner Ryan went on to review the techniques used by each of these commands, some of them in common but others more relevant to the command's particular function. Surveillance, both physical and by electronic means is widely used by each of them as appropriate, as is the skilled analysis of material collected by the various means. Whilst the *Special Projects Unit* is closely allied to the New South Wales Crime Commission in the fight against organised crime, it also enhances the investigative capabilities of the *Internal Affairs* command by the use of its resources and methods. *Integrity Testing* is aimed at officers who have been identified as being possibly corrupt or engaged in serious misconduct or criminal activity. Intelligence is an essential tool in this field and analysts consider a whole range of information, including the subject's financial activities and any past history of complaint against him or her. *Integrity Testing* has been defined as :

> "... the creation of a situation where an officer who is believed to be committing serious misconduct or criminal behaviour can be observed. The situation is designed to test whether the officer responds in a corrupt or unethical manner ..."

The *Covert Unit's* responsibilities are many and varied, but it is frequently used as an adjunct to the work of the other units, having the experience of undercover operations and surveillance by all modern techniques. Commissioner Ryan continued:

> "The level of competence of an investigator is a major

consideration when recruiting potential investigators for the Internal Affairs command, yet more importantly is their ability to embrace new methods and apply creative thinking to their investigations. Previously, internal investigation techniques and methodologies were primitive and ineffective, for example:

- failure to carry out impartial investigations, or pursue misconduct allegations with the same rigour or approach as seen in ordinary criminal investigations;
- lack of security in relation to corruption investigations, leading to a compromise;
- ineffective investigative techniques;
- investigations frequently starting and ending with an officer's denial of the allegations;
- investigations into serious misconduct closing once minor disciplinary infraction was established; and
- lack of protection and support for internal informants."

A useful measure of the results of this new approach to police misconduct can be seen in statistics showing that of 477 officers nominated for consideration of having lost the Commissioner's confidence, no less than 196 left the service and, at the time of Mr Ryan's paper, 72 cases were still under consideration.

A useful weapon in the Australian armoury was forged in the passage of the Police Integrity Commission Act 1996, section 5 (Appendix 4), which allows disciplinary action against officers who have left the service. Many officers who found themselves under suspicion took the opportunity to take medical discharge or retirement, thus putting an end to their liability for penalty. In contrast, UK officers can be dealt with at the discretion of the Home Secretary on the Chief Officer's recommendation who has, as in the case of Inspector Field in the 19th century, control over the grant or discontinuance of pension rights.

Police service history shows a past peppered with reforms, restarts and initiatives. Some, as in the earlier attempts in Australia to curb corruption, have not scratched the surface of a long standing problem; whilst others have begun well but sooner or later run out of steam. In Britain, the best efforts of Metropolitan Commissioners such as Sir Robert Mark and Sir Paul Condon have had their measure of success in rooting out criminal officers and either bringing them to justice or getting rid of them. However, at best, they were only able to create a relatively short respite from a cancerous growth of dishonesty, whose cells remain embedded in the organisation. If proof were needed of this contention, one need look no further than recent cases coming before the courts, in which the underlying facts bear a strong likeness to trials of the past.

In April 2000, *The News of the World* newspaper reported that a Detective Constable McGuiness, having pleaded guilty to burglary, conspiring to supply cannabis, perverting the course of justice and receiving stolen money, was sentenced to nine years' imprisonment He was described by prosecution counsel as having turned "supergrass" to expose a "culture of corruption" in the Flying Squad, and he spoke of an incident in which £14,000 in notes was found in a criminal's house, under the bed, during a search. The officer apparently turned to the other Detectives saying "Christmas has come early", and allowed them to help themselves, but keeping £2,000 for himself. The cash was counted and the exact amount in forged notes put in its place. Other incidents were described, including an occasion when a thief's girl friend, disgusted with his criminal behaviour, threw a large sum of stolen money into a ditch. Members of the Flying Squad found it and McGuiness, during a visit to a senior officer's house, saw the banknotes being dried out. McGuiness's career came to an end when CIB2 set a trap by putting £200,000 worth of cannabis into a house, and with a secreted camera recorded him and another Detective break in and steal it. In mitigation Mr John Coffey, QC, told the Judge that the defendant had no choice but to join in the thieving. He said: "It was often instigated and orchestrated by senior officers. You fell in with it or your career came to an end".

In 1999, two experienced criminals were convicted at the Old Bailey of, among other matters, an armed robbery for which they were sentenced to 17 years each. They appealed against their conviction on the grounds that two Flying Squad officers had fabricated the evidence against them, and the Court of Appeal granted a retrial. When it came before Judge Geoffrey Grigson for trial by a fresh jury, counsel for the Crown applied to conduct the case without the two officers who were facing corruption charges or (*sic*) disciplinary investigation, and to rely on a statement concerning disciplinary investigations into them. Unsurprisingly, the Judge refused to allow a sanitised version of their evidence to go before the jury and the case fell to the ground. Whilst it would be quite wrong to draw the firm conclusion that the officers were guilty of any impropriety with regard to the appellants, the fact that experienced counsel did not feel able to call them to give evidence leaves an aura of doubt over the case.

On May 15, 2000, the London *Daily Telegraph* reported that "Fifty-two police officers have been removed from the élite National Crime Squad since it was created two years ago, amid allegations of corruption and malpractice. Up to 10 have been 'sent back' to their home forces on suspicion of collaborating with criminals and others have been accused of offences ranging from losing vital evidence to overtime fraud."

Politicians who find themselves or their party under attack when some major scandal breaks are fond of platitudes such as "lessons will be learned" and "measures will be put into place", when the lessons have been open for learning, perhaps for years. And "Measures being put into place" has a distinct ring of Alice in Wonderland, in that the phrase means whatever the speaker wants it to mean, if anything.

There is no room for such weasel words, nor room for complacency in the maintenance of police integrity, and never a time when it can be said with confidence, that corruption is under control.

Chapter 18

Sexual Crimes

A substantial part of the Woods Royal Commission's inquiries and final report were taken up by the subject of paedophiles and allegations that the police had protected offenders from prosecution. Whilst there had been a great deal of speculation, rumour and innuendo circulating in the press about senior people supposedly involved in a variety of sexual crimes whilst under police protection, nothing of substance had become public. This situation changed dramatically when Colin Fisk, a paedophile of many years standing, and his co-defendant Detective Constable Larry Churchill, were, in March 1989, remanded in custody to await trial for drugs offences. He and Churchill had been arrested following the successful "Operation Hawkesbury" referred to in Chapter 14. Fisk, an admitted sexual deviant, became upset with some of his associates because they had not visited him whilst in custody, and he made allegations against them claiming that they, like himself, had had sexual relationships with children. He went on to say that a group of police officers had for years protected them from prosecution and had engaged in extortion and fraud. He named a Senior Detective Sergeant as one of those officers and Churchill as being another. The allegations were so serious that the Internal Police Security Branch (IPSB) formed a task force under the title "Operation Gull", monitored by the ICAC, to investigate the allegations.

Coincidentally, a police investigation, code-named "Operation Seabeach", was looking into allegations that the proprietors of a children's nursery and two others had been involved in the sexual abuse of young children. In the course of his disclosures, Fisk named the officer in charge of that inquiry as one of those prepared to provide protection for him and his associates. Later, when inquiries into the whole matter became the responsibility of the Royal Commission, the officer gave evidence on oath and denied the allegations.

In 1993, Fisk co-operated in a television broadcast, repeating his allegations of a police cover-up for paedophiles which led to a public inquiry being set up by the ICAC: included in its terms of reference was a request to examine allegations that police had protected paedophiles from investigation and prosecution. There was considerable overlap between the ICAC and Royal Commission's briefs and on December 1, 1994, responsibility for the matter passed to the Royal Commission. The ICAC at that time did not have a permanent head following the expiry of Mr Ian Tenby, QC's, term of office, and Mr John Mant was filling in as caretaker for a two month period. Requests to the Government for the urgent appointment of a new head together with requests for necessary funding appear to have gone unanswered, with the result that the organisation was wholly under-resourced for such a massive undertaking.

The report by those involved in "Operation Gull" concluded that corruption had existed in the way officers had been dealing with paedophiles until March 1989, but that there was no evidence of its continuation until April, 1992, when the report was published.

In August 1994, Fisk gave a version of events to a newspaper reporter in which he promised to reveal to the Royal Commission the names of businessmen, media personalities, senior legal figures and politicians who were involved in paedophile or pederast activities. He claimed to be in fear of assassination at the instance of a ring of millionaires involved in child corruption and their police protectors, but later retracted almost all he had said. His lack of consistency did not augur well for any firm legal action based solely upon his words, but the seeds of suspicion had been well sown.

The Commission could not confine itself to allegations against the police alone because the subject was, and is, far too complicated for such a simplistic approach. It had first to define paedophilia and pederasty within its terms of reference, which it did as:

> "... taking paedophiles to mean those adults who act on their sexual urge for children, in a manner which is contrary to the laws of the State of New South Wales and pederast as being taken to mean a paedophile who engages in homosexual intercourse with a boy, who similarly is below the age of consent ...",

then to review the work of agencies whose concern should have been to protect children from the activities of those who would abuse them. Each agency was found to have its own views on how to deal with the problem, and each its own practices in regard to co-operation with other concerned bodies. In many instances that co-operation was non-existent and, in practice, one body's efforts to act in the best interests of child victims was frustrated by another's. Where the welfare of children within their sphere of responsibility should have been their first priority, that was frequently subordinated to the protection of the agency itself or individuals within its ranks.

One case study reported by the Commission in its final report concerned a child who, from the age of eight became subject to continuing sexual abuse by the eldest of her brothers over many years, until she reached the age of 15 years in 1984. The matter was brought to the attention of the then Department of Community Services (DCS) prior to 1984 as the result of information from a school counsellor. In 1984, the girl complained that the younger of her two brothers had also been abusing her since she was 12 years old. The girl's father was a police officer and having become aware of her complaints, informed DCS workers that his youngest son, himself a serving police officer, had admitted to him that her complaints were true. The girl was placed into care but because she was reluctant to follow up her complaint the DCS took the decision not to prosecute. The father told DCS staff that his policeman son had confessed to a priest and was being counselled by him; this assurance apparently satisfying the authority that they need take no further action.

One can see why the father had been relieved at the decision taken by the DCS, in all probability confident that his sons' misconduct would not be repeated now that it had come into the open, particularly in view of the likely reaction of the police authorities should they come to hear of it. The DCS did not interview either of the brothers, nor did they report the matter to the police or make any significant inquiry to confirm the girl's accusations. Thus it was that the police were denied an opportunity to investigate this matter and to become aware of a child sexual abuser in the community, regardless of whether or not a prosecution could have been launched. Nor were they aware that the abuser was within their own ranks and working in the field of child protection 13 years after the offences when all was revealed before the Commission. The Commission then discovered that parents of some children who were under the wing of the police child protection service as victims of sexual misbehaviour, were claiming that the same officer had handled those complaints "inappropriately". Whilst it is right to say that these complaints were, in the main unsubstantiated, the DCS's failure to notify was an opportunity missed to bring a potentially damaging situation to an end.

After such a long delay, it was difficult for the Commission to come to a precise reason for the DCS having taken such a weak view of this particular case, but there remains a suspicion that this was an example of "turf warfare" in which the authority was too busy defending its own position against another. The NSW Child Advocate, in a footnote to the Commission's report states that ... "turf protection is a complex problem, caused by the different approaches and philosophies of the departments involved ... the whole police system is regarded with suspicion by welfare and the whole welfare is regarded with some suspicion by the police system. The health system regards them all with suspicion because they are different philosophies and many doctors think that this is not a medical but a social problem, and so on". It hardly needs saying that energy expended in protecting one's own system and philosophies, which ought to be directed for the benefit of the public, is a disgrace.

***

In 1996, the DCS supplied a number of files to the Commission concerning allegations of sexual abuse made against its own employees; in many instances they proved accurate and, on any reading of those files, those employees should never have been involved in the care of young people.

In one instance, a young single man was the subject of complaints spread over a period of six years concerning his relationships with 14- and 15-year-old children in his care. At one stage, having received an anonymous letter of complaint against the young man the Public Service Board referred it to the DCS for attention and some months later, following the matter up, asked what the result had been. The papers in the case appeared to have been lost, but the Public Service Board was told that there seemed to be no substance to the complaint and therefore no further action would be required. Between then and 1989, more complaints of a similar nature were received against him until, following an internal inquiry, his salary was reduced but without any further discernible penalty. Even this reduction was soon reviewed and his salary level restored, but in September 1990 the employee wisely accepted the offer of a discharge on medical grounds. Not satisfied with this merciful outcome the employee later demanded, and got, an assurance from the DCS that all records of the matter would be removed from his personal file and destroyed. The DCS baulked at a further request that he be given a reference, but nevertheless supplied him, instead, with a certificate of having served but retired for medical reasons.

Thus he was able to leave the service with neither stain on his character nor a question mark against his suitability to be employed with children. The police were not informed of the relatively serious criminal complaints made against him. The investigation by the DCS was inept and shallow as far as can be ascertained from belatedly reported facts, and its decision to give a certificate of service in the terms it did was an affront to common sense and justice.

***

There were many stories floating about in the press and among politicians and lawyers, that some senior figures in the legal establishment were active and persistent paedophiles. It was also suggested that their activities were being covered up by police officers for unspecified reasons. Such a situation was theoretically possible and, if true, the reasons for doing so could very well centre around the awe in which highly placed individuals are held by many police officers of all ranks. It is easy to understand the apprehension felt by a lowly officer who has been given the task of investigating complaints against a respected person of public renown, because the temptation to doubt the complaint simply because someone of the individual's position and status is unlikely to misbehave is very strong. On the other hand there can be a natural temptation to carry out deliberately superficial investigations, believing that the target is invulnerable and capable of exacting a damaging reaction. An example this kind of problem and perhaps of this kind of thinking can be found in the case of the late David Yeldham, a former Supreme Court Justice, who took his own life in November 1996.

The Royal Commission was informed in 1995 by the police, that criminal conduct was being alleged by an informer against a retired Judge. The informer was interviewed by the Commission and repeated a story told him by a friend who had seen Mr Yeldham at Wynyard railway station, in some difficulty over an allegation of sexual misconduct. The Commission instituted general inquiries into Mr Yeldham, and instructed the police to produce whatever information they were holding about him in their files. Gradually, with evidence from police officers and examination of such papers as they were able to produce, a comprehensive and disturbing picture of his activities began to emerge.

David Albert Yeldham had been called to the NSW Bar in 1955 and was appointed Queen's Counsel in 1972. In 1974 he was appointed a Judge in the NSW Supreme Court, where he served with distinction until his retirement in 1990. As a Judge, he was regarded as a reserved man who gave sound judgments, never displaying the irritation or petulance that has marked so many of those who spend time on the bench passing judgment on others. A family man with children he was, on the surface, entirely normal in his life and attitudes to people.

The earliest incidents which came to notice were those from a witness, referred to by the Commission as CC13, who spoke of meeting Mr Yeldham on a train in the 1960s when he was 15 years of age. Mr Yeldham, then a young barrister, had masturbated in front of him and given him some money, after which they had met again on a number of occasions in Yeldham's chambers where sexual acts took place.

On December 12, 1988, Mr Yeldham was arrested at Central Station when, with an adult male, he was seen in what was delicately described as "compromising circumstances" and a note was made in police records, although no charges resulted from this incident.

In 1996, the witness CC13 took Commission investigators to Wynyard station where he identified the scene and pointed out the place where, in 1990, he had seen Mr Yeldham being interviewed by police. He was being spoken to concerning a complaint made by a young man who worked on a nearby news stand. An intelligence report from the police confirmed that such an incident had been investigated, and that a copy of the report was sent to Special Branch. The Special Branch Commander's notes, when they were finally given to the Commission, showed that the incident concerned "suspected acts of indecency"; that Mr Yeldham had been interviewed, but having denied the allegations, no prosecution followed. Investigators for the Commission tracked down the youth concerned in the Wynyard Station incident, and having examined him on oath had to decide on how to proceed with the inquiry.

The Commission's conclusion was, that if the evidence of the youth and the witness CC13 were accurate, it must follow that a number of police officers had at various times given false accounts of their part in the matter. The question requiring an answer was: had there been conspiracy at high level to protect Mr Yeldham from public exposure of his behaviour, involving the Special Branch, senior police officers, the judiciary and the executive? The incidents described in this chapter were just some of those in which this man was involved over many years, and it is now clear that he was not stopped due to the failure of those in authority to act with courage, efficiency and propriety. Special Branch officers who had evidence of the late Judge's propensities must shoulder the heaviest burden, if only because they were clearly intermeddling with matters outside their department's proper terms of reference, instead of leaving the matter to those whose responsibility it was. For the ordinary police officer who had the misfortune to become involved with allegations against a man of high judicial position, the hand of Special Branch and its mysterious ways must have been heavy indeed.

On October 31, 1996, Mrs Franca Arena, a backbencher, under the protection of parliamentary privilege, named the retired Justice as one who had been given special treatment by the Commission in not publicising the fact that they were inquiring into his behaviour. Yeldham telephoned the Commission after learning of Mrs Arena's revelations before Parliament and having admitted that he had indeed been involved in illicit sexual acts, made an appointment to see them on the next day, but on the afternoon of that day was found inside his car in the garage of the family home, dead from carbon monoxide poisoning.

As a result of Mrs Arena's statement, Justice Wood found himself having to defend his cautious approach to publicity in respect of those appearing before the Commission. One journalist, under the caption Suicide Toll, named "Two accused paedophiles, two policemen, a former Judge and one other witness", as those who had killed themselves after appearing before or having been named adversely before the Commission. Justice Wood's approach was vindicated upon publication of the report which demonstrated a high degree of sensitivity among its other attributes. By then, of course, the hysterical and unfair accusations against him were long in the past.

***

From about 1975, the police at Wollongong became aware of stories circulating about a Mr Bevan, then Mayor, and his sexual activities with young men. A very wealthy man, he was considered to be the proverbial pillar of local society as an alderman, businessman and public benefactor. However, his sexual propensities were firmly orientated towards young men and boys from 11 to 18 years of age. In 1982, an 11-year-old boy was interviewed by officers and told a story of numerous indecent assaults by Bevan, culminating in buggery on the last occasion. He named another boy who had been subjected to similar treatment, but when police interviewed that boy, he completely denied that any such activity had taken place. The Detective engaged in the case interviewed Anthony Bevan, who denied any impropriety, with the result that the officer was obliged to submit a report saying that there was insufficient evidence to proceed against him.

In 1983, three boys between 10 and 13 years told the police that a man for whom they were doing small jobs, sexually assaulted them. He then took them to see Bevan and although there was apparently no complaint against him, the police saw fit to record that Bevan was a "well known homo and paedophile".

In 1990, police officers had occasion to talk to a number of boys who gave information about "Tony" [Bevan], strongly suggesting that he and a partner were enticing boys and young men into sexual practices with them by supplying drugs and following this up by a form of blackmail. Intelligence reports were filed by the investigating officer but no follow up inquiries were made, either of the boys named, or of Bevan.

In 1990, Detective Sergeant King submitted a report on Bevan and a group of his associates, who were alleged to be involved in sexual offences against young males. It was claimed that visitors to parties at Bevan's apartment were charged a sum of money for the benefit of a session with one or other of the boys. In addition, Bevan had made a video recording of sexual acts with a boy whom he had earlier assaulted. Sergeant King's report reviewed all the matters previously alleged against Bevan and, having carried out the proper procedures, expected that a full investigation would be launched. No such investigation took place and the Sergeant was told by his senior officer that his information would be of no value if a prosecution was put in hand.

The Royal Commission appeared to have little difficulty in tracing witnesses and assembling a damning case against Bevan years after the police had, apparently, swept the whole matter under the carpet. Nor did Commission investigators have too much trouble in discovering a series of telex messages which, although phrased in a way intended to mask the parties and the subject, proved to be communications between Bevan and his various willing victims. Had it not been for Bevan's death in 1991 and the deaths of some of his associates, there would have been ample evidence available to launch a successful prosecution. The Commission refrained from making any suggestion that there has been a corrupt collusion between the police and Bevan. In the absence of corruption in the accepted sense, one must draw the conclusion that a wariness about becoming involved in targeting such a high profile figure persuaded police officers of considerable rank to avoid what was a clear duty to investigate the matter properly.

***

In the paedophile section of its final report, the commissioner's conclusions can be summarised quite shortly in that:

> "there were police prepared to implement corrupt arrangements with paedophiles, or to stand over them with a view to extortion; and the paedophiles concerned were particularly vulnerable to such approaches and were sufficiently well organised to arrange for favoured treatment through an intermediary."

The New York Police Department
United States of America

The City of New York Commission to Investigate Allegations of Police Corruption and Anti-corruption Procedures of the Police Department

Chapter 19

Intoxicating Liquor & its Effect on Corruption

In 1783, when the British troops and their Hessian mercenaries marched out of New York to be replaced by George Washington's American army, the detritus of George III's forces who had chosen to remain rather than make the weary journey to Newfoundland, became a serious challenge to the city's peace and tranquillity. Washington, however, wrote the following letter to the President of Congress on December 3, 1783:

> "On November 25 the British troops left this city, and a detachment of our army marched into it. The civil power was immediately put in possession, and I have the happiness to assure you, that the most perfect regularity and good order have prevailed ever since."

It may be that Washington had drifted a little from his famed truthfulness; or perhaps had relied too much on the assurances of others, because contemporary reports suggest a high degree of lawlessness existed within the city. However, the efforts of his troops, together with the creation of a civilian watch system, provided the embryo policing system which eventually, after the tragedy of the civil war and the 1863 riots, became the New York Police Department. Those riots were in protest against the compulsory drafting of men into the Union army; usually the poorest who could not afford to pay hundreds of dollars to buy exemption. The rioters very soon overwhelmed the authorities and by the end of the disturbances an orphanage for black children had been burned out; a number of black men had been lynched and three police officers lay dead.

The Department's Roll of Honour now bears the names of nearly 600 officers who gave their lives in the execution of their duty, a majority having been killed by criminals and many dying in the act of rescuing others. Their names, stemming from almost every country in Europe and South America, demonstrate the ethnic mix of its members, with those of Irish extraction figuring prominently together with Hispanics, Germans and other Europeans from nations large and small. Many of their forefathers had been persuaded to come by the blandishments of ship owners and agents who, with advertisements posted on quaysides, offered cheap passage to the New World and all its wonderful opportunities. In reality, many found themselves aboard overloaded "coffin ships" whose masters had little regard for their safety and welfare, but more for the profit in filling spare capacity with a miserable human cargo.

On landing in New York, ill and often near to starving, they fell prey to dockside touts who proceeded to separate them from what little property they had. The promised milk and honey only came, if at all, with good luck and grindingly hard work: for some it was a poverty as bad as the one they left behind. Some, probably those with a basic education, eventually became police officers, often with their sons and grandchildren following in their footsteps.

The NYPD's Roll of Honour is testament to the bravery and dedication of its staff since the Department was formed, and continuing until this day. However, as with all good there often comes a dark side and the Department's dark side is a long history of intermittent and serious corruption.

In-fighting between political parties and pressures from powerful special interest groups must take some blame for creating that dark side as can be illustrated by the passage in Congress of a law prohibiting the production of beer and spirits during the Great War of 1914-18, and its inevitable consequences. This law hardened into the 18th Amendment to the Constitution, effective in January 1920, which prohibited export, import, manufacture, sale or transportation of intoxicating liquors. Instead of transforming America into a nation of abstemious and law-abiding people as its lobbyists had expected, it had quite the reverse effect because the demand for drink increased and there were criminals ready to satisfy that demand. Opportunities for corruption over the whole of the USA resulted in police officers falling to the golden temptations held out by rum-runners, bootleggers and criminal organisations. It had been calculated that during Prohibition, $2,000,000,000 worth of trade was passed from the previously legitimate outlets of brewers, distillers and retailers into the hands of criminal gangs who lavished money on police and politicians at every level to protect themselves from prosecution.

In the early 1970s the force had hit such a low ebb that public opinion demanded that something be done about an organisation in which some of its members were once more allying themselves to professional criminals engaged in illegal betting and gaming, just as an earlier generation had done with the beer barons of the Prohibition era. The then Mayor set up the Knapp Commission to examine and report on what had gone wrong and what could be done about it. As a result of the Commission's inquiries, the then

Commissioner of Police, Patrick V. Murphy, set up an Internal Affairs Department (IAD), whose primary function was to investigate complaints of serious corruption against officers throughout the whole Police Department. To give an element of local control and responsibility Field Internal Affairs Units (FIAU) were set up in each patrol borough and specialist command which were intended to deal with lesser forms of misbehaviour under the supervision of the local commander, but with access to assistance and advice from IAD when necessary. The system worked well in the early years, but, as so often happens, a gradual decline set in until, by the 1980s, corruption was as bad as ever but with narcotics providing the profit base from which bribes could be paid.

On July 24, 1992, the Hon. David N. Dinkins, Mayor of New York, signed Executive Order No. 42, establishing a Commission to investigate allegations of corruption in the police department and to examine its procedures. Judge Milton Mollen was appointed to head the Commission and its final report was submitted to the Mayor on July 7, 1994. An interesting fact to emerge from the Commission's inquiries was that a consistent cycle of corruption covered a period of about 20 years - almost exactly the interval between Knapp and Mollen.

The most prominent character whose activities created much of the need for a major inquiry, was Michael Dowd, a police officer in the high crime 75th Precinct, in the Brooklyn North Patrol Borough. Over a period of six years, no less than 16 complaints had been filed against Dowd and some members of a group of his police associates, none of which had resulted in either criminal or departmental charges, despite lengthy and vigorous work by Sergeant Joseph Trimboli of the Brooklyn North FIAU. The complaints included theft, robbery and supplying drugs among other matters, but every case against Dowd was filed as unsubstantiated and it was only after his arrest by officers of the Suffolk County Police on drugs charges that matters came to a head. The Mollen Commission reviewed some of crimes of Dowd and his co-conspirators in the course of its final report, exposing massive failures of command which had allowed their depredations to continue for so long.

It was in the spring of 1986, that the 7th Precinct's Commander reported to the local FIAU that Dowd and a colleague had been stealing money from a number of people including drugs' offenders, prisoners and even from the effects of dead bodies. Instead of such serious allegations being investigated by the IAD who should have known about and undertaken the inquiry, it was left to Sergeant Trimboli of the FIAU with his inadequate resources to get on with it. Within days of learning of these complaints against Dowd, IAD piled further work on Trimboli with orders to investigate additional allegations, this time of brutality by Dowd and several of his associates. Trimboli was later to tell the Commission that throughout his abortive efforts to bring Dowd to justice during more than five years, his requests for help and better facilities from IAD were either ignored or sidelined. He told the Commission that his equipment consisted of a camera, a pair of binoculars and a paper shredder; hardly the weaponry of an organised and motivated task force. The only effect of the complaint and investigation was that Dowd and his associates were temporarily transferred by the Borough Chief to Coney Island for the summer months, no doubt to the temporary relief of his senior officers and the local drugs dealers who had been paying him off.

A set of premises, the R&T Grocery became pivotal to the Commission's work in due course. Situated in the 75th Precinct area, it was, subsidiary to its ostensible business, a location where drugs traders operated and, on a summer's evening, three police officers committed an armed robbery on the premises. One of them, Officer Walter Yurkiw, left the car which had been used in the crime at a car park near the 75th Precinct with property stolen from R&T Grocers in full view on the seat, and then reported to the precinct to begin his day's duty. Yurkiw was very soon arrested by Captain Friedland, Commander of the local FIAU, but next day the IAD appointed one of its own investigators, Captain Thomas Callaghan, to take over from the local man with instructions to contain his investigation within the narrow bounds of an isolated armed robbery. Friedland suspected that Dowd, Yurkiw and other officers had been engaging in extensive corruption and other crimes during the preceding two years and this robbery was only part of a much wider picture. To limit the robbery investigation without considering the wider scene made no sense to him. That Dowd in particular was leading a flamboyant life, flouting a new Corvette car, expensive clothes and a capacity to fund lavish parties and trips to gambling venues for some of his colleagues, confirmed Friedland's suspicions without providing the essential hard evidence. A disturbing feature of events at this time was the certainty that many of Dowd's senior officers were fully aware of his scale of spending and also had good reason to suspect the source of his income yet did nothing about it. Worse! He was rated on his performance in 1987 and part of the comments read: "This officer could excel within the New York City Police Department and easily become a role model for others to emulate if he maximised his inner drive to fulfil job responsibilities to the fullest".

Over a period of six years, Trimboli pursued his inquiries into Dowd and others involved in corruption and associated crimes. All complaints were filed with IAD against Dowd and each one was allocated to Trimboli to investigate as isolated incidents and all were closed by IAD by agreement with the Borough Commander as "inconclusive", quite contrary to the weight of Trimboli's evidence and recommendations. The failure of Trimboli's efforts, the extent of Dowd's criminality, and the reasons for his virtual immunity were described in Justice Mollen's final report.

* * *

The Commission took evidence from a large number of people including officers of all ranks, private citizens, lawyers and informers; the basic picture emerging from these sources, including admissions from Dowd himself was that Precinct 75, despite having a core of honest personnel, was riddled with corruption. Dowd and his associates both inside and outside the force were committing armed robberies, targeting drugs dealers in order to steal cash, drugs and anything else of value that they might find whilst at the same time leaving the field clear for favoured dealers.

Not all dealers were his targets, because some were participants in the robberies, whilst others bought the stolen drugs to recycle in their own businesses. Two informers, members of a drug gang under the control of a man named Adam Diaz, a native of the Dominican Republic, revealed that Dowd was paid between $3,000 and $4,000 and an ounce of cocaine each week, frequently going to a known drugs location in uniform on duty to collect his dues. For these regular payments, Diaz was given a large measure of police protection and the assistance of Dowd as a drugs courier. As well as Dowd, there were up to 25 officers taking part in some of these crimes at various times, but a hard core of about a dozen were the most regularly active.

Dowd's audacity had no bounds and he told the Commission of an incident in which he and his partner, Kenneth Eurell, attended a reported shooting outside their proper area, accurately suspecting that the location was a drugs venue. They were the first officers on the scene and went into the house, virtually stepping over the victim's body in a search for drugs or cash. Having found a stash of heroin and a pistol, Dowd put them into a duffle bag and they left the incident for others to deal with, none of whom including a Sergeant, questioned their presence or activities. Perhaps the most serious aspect of this whole sorry catalogue of offending was the way in which he and the other crooked officers were allowed to get away with it for such a long time.

* * *

We have seen that in the aftermath of the Knapp Commissions report, an investigative and control system was set up, with IAD as the primary command and FIAUs dealing with investigation in local patrol boroughs. It appears that whilst the organisation was in its first flush of enthusiasm and under the watchful eye of the then Police Commissioner, it worked very well. That initial enthusiasm and sharpness aimed at the control and elimination of corruption turned, in time, to a condition bordering upon lethargy. Worse was to follow when its *raison d'être* changed from control and elimination to one of preventing exposure to the public gaze of large scale corruption. Its members sought to achieve this object by fragmenting the overall picture into individual complaints and either ignoring or concealing vital links to others. The R&T Grocery store robbery case is an example of this approach; an investigation which it will be remembered, was taken out of Captain Friedland's hands and passed to Captain Callaghan of IAD.

Every local police group, whether it be called a precinct, station or squad, and in whatever country, acquires a mine of information about crimes and likely perpetrators in the neighbourhood and in the case of the 75th Precinct all that knowledge was either in the possession of or was readily available to IAD should they wish to use it. There was plenty of information on record about Dowd and his associates, in particular his friendship with Yurkiw who was now in custody for the robbery. Over the following weeks, even more information was funnelled into IAD demonstrating the close connection between Dowd, his associates and the robbery with its drugs connotations, yet

IAD maintained its position and continued to treat the robbery as an isolated crime requiring no extraneous complications. It was about as effective as trying to complete a difficult jig-saw puzzle but steadfastly refusing to look at the box lid. It was so much easier to record a complaint as "unsubstantiated" when it could be quietly shelved if it were treated in isolation, rather than attempting uncover interlinking evidence of similar complaints against the same officers.

This reluctance to accept the clear and provable links between the numerous robberies appeared to the Commission to have started high in the Police Commissioner's office, filtering down to the lower ranks for one overriding reason - fear of adverse public opinion and its potential effect on careers! The thinking was that if an isolated incident of police misbehaviour became public knowledge, it may well be reasonable to point this out as an example of the Police Commissioner's determination to stamp out corruption. If, on the other hand, 25 officers are arrested for various linked crimes, as happened in 1977 in the 77th Precinct, the careers of those who should have prevented such a situation arising are put very firmly in jeopardy. In the wake of the 77th Precinct scandal, the Precinct Commander was demoted and moved; a Chief, two Captains, seven Lieutenants and 14 Sergeants were transferred to other places with serious detriment to their future prospects in the service. In the cold light of hindsight, many of them must have regretted their inertia when faced with the unpalatable truth that they were ruling over a nest of entrenched corruption became public. This is well documented in the Commission's report of evidence given before it by men in command positions:

> "The department didn't want the publicity ..." "Why, didn't they chip off one, two, three or four [officers] and it wouldn't have made a big thing instead of making a wholesale arrest of four, five, six officers - you take one here, one there ... and it don't make headlines" and
>
> "The message that when out to the field was that maybe we shouldn't be so aggressive in fighting corruption because the Department just does not want a bad press ..."

An absence of enthusiasm for proper investigation, for whatever motive, was serious enough, but the active discouragement and obstruction applied to Sergeant Trimboli's efforts appears to have been far worse. As an FIAU investigator whose cases were allocated to him by his IAD superiors, he was entitled to rely upon their full assistance and support. Instead, already overloaded with cases, he was made to submit work sheets to IAD at weekly intervals. By looking at these work sheets, IAD officers were able to monitor Trimboli's progress and to use the intelligence and hard evidence he was gathering. That evidence and intelligence was building up into a convincing case against Dowd and his crew, but although all this information was put before Captain Callaghan in Trimboli's work sheets by Lieutenant Hoteling of the IAD staff, Callaghan chose to ignore it. He said that it had nothing to do with his case and that he did not want so see any more of them. And so it was that gems of information linking Dowd to that and other such robberies were, until revealed to the Commission, totally lost. In a similar vein, information which would have been invaluable to Trimboli in his investigations was never passed to him from IAD; one particularly potent item came to his knowledge for the first time when in the course of his discussions with the Commission they told him of it.

The IAD could hardly claim pressure of work as a reason for its indolence because the Commission's research showed that 95% of cases referred to it were sent to FIAUs for investigation, and of the 5% retained within IAD, more than a quarter of them were of such a minor character that they could properly have been dealt with by the offender's Sergeant.

* * *

One aspect of the Mollen report which had not been touched upon by past Commissions was that of police violence and unjustified brutality. Commissioner Mollen felt that corruption and brutality frequently ran hand in hand and that, logically, they should be investigated together by his own and future Commissions. He considered that whilst corruption was usually about money or valuables, brutality was an abuse of power and the distinction between them could sometimes be unclear. Examples of this link were given by reference to a former officer, Alfonso Compress, who, whilst in uniform and busily robbing a dealer of his cocaine stock, shot him in the abdomen with his service revolver. Dowd, in his evidence to the Commission conceded that, "They [police officers] who are taking money will more typically be ones that are giving beatings, yes". Whilst there may be many reasons for officers beating people without there being a connection with corruption for gain, the Commission's researches showed that a sample of 234 officers who were considered corrupt or corruptible were five times more likely to have five or more unnecessary force allegations against them than those in a randomly selected control group of the same magnitude.

* * *

In 1995, the Mayor, Rudolph W. Giuliani, established the Commission to Combat Police Corruption, providing its powers by Executive Order No. 18. One of its principal objects is to have an agency, independent of the police department, to oversee efforts being made to break the [20 year] cycle of recurring corruption. Its objectives are to monitor: all aspects of the NYPD's anti-corruption policies and procedures which relate to corruption controls, the NYPD's investigative efforts into corruption allegations, and the prevailing culture within the NYPD that allows or disallows corruption to continue. In addition, the Commission examines the effectiveness of the NYPD's overall efforts to improve its anti-corruption programmes and to increase the integrity of the entire NYPD.

In order to carry out its task, the Commission scrutinises investigations into specific corruption allegations with authority contained in the Executive Order to request "any and all documents, records, reports, files or other information relating to any matter within the jurisdiction of the Commission, except such documents as cannot be so disclosed according to law".

* * *

The Mollen Commission's report is a model of hard-hitting and relentless exposure of a failing police administration and its anti-corruption system. Measures of correction and control were set up in the wake of the report, in particular the element of independent inspection and monitoring, but also other practical methods of bringing the Department's small but dangerous elements under control, particularly in the field of brutality. There have been set-backs in recent years - the horrendous story of a group of officers assaulting a Haitian immigrant named Abner Louima which culminated in his being sodomised with a broom handle; and the killing of a Guinean street trader by four officers who fired at him 41 times, hitting him with 19 bullets. There have also been incidents of corruption for gain, but in common with every other police service, regardless of what measures are put into force, such incidents can never be entirely eliminated.

For how long the re-start in the NYPD can be effectively sustained will be for the future to decide.

Chapter 20

Institutional Crime - An Overview

The past chapters have been an attempt to review the most damaging instances of corruption in three large modern police services, apart from some minor deviations from that general purpose, with the object of providing a starting point for those who have general interest in the topic as well as those concerned with containing the problem. The deeper one probes into past examples of corruption, the more one is surprised by the similarity in origin and development of unlawful behaviour by a particular arm of two of them, namely the Metropolitan and the New South Wales police and their detectives. The NYPD, at least within a limited time span and geographical area shows many similarities of activity, but with uniformed patrolmen as the people concerned. As we have seen, the Metropolitan Police Detective history began with a small group of skilled investigators which, after the first reorganisation, became the Criminal Investigation Department or as it is universally known, the CID. In time the CID split, amoeba-like, into specialist departments with particular skills and responsibilities although still under the general banner of the department.

In New South Wales, the beginnings of organised criminal investigation followed a similar pattern, but under the name Criminal Investigation Bureau or CIB. It appears that the CIB was even more élitist than the CID until the closing years of its reign when, in 1987, it was dismantled and its members devolved to regional crime squads; that spirit of élitism followed them to their new postings where they rapidly corrupted some of their new colleagues. The same defensive closing of ranks and culture of silence was still evident after the devolvement, and still varied little in its solidarity from that in the CID. Differences between the two services can be seen, of course, but that may be as a result of the rather diffident approach to public linen-washing in Britain as against the stark public revelations of the Wood and Mollen Commission reports.

In the UK Parliament, whenever some major tragedy or scandal arises, Opposition members will frequently seize upon it as a new stick with which to beat the Government of the day and, between calls for a Minister's resignation, demand a public inquiry. The Government, when forced into a corner, however, find the appointment of a Royal Commission to be a more attractive option because such reports often finish up in one of Whitehall's pigeon holes, usually long after those who set it in motion no longer hold positions of power. Such Commissions only rarely have a significant impact on events, but whilst a Commission investigation into the police and the CID in particular could be a worthwhile project, it would be difficult to match Justice Wood's far-reaching and incisive document.

In New York, with a political structure which puts the police under the direct control of the Mayor and his officials, the Mayor may well be tempted to rule with an eye on the next election with the result that, when public opinion dictates, he must be seen to do something to deal with problems. One product of this situation was the appointment of the Mollen Commission with its willingness to conduct much of its work in public. Thus one can read the testimony at public hearings of a variety of witnesses, including self-confessedly dishonest police officers and of higher ranks who were obliged to air their incompetent management for all to hear. It must be said, however, that the setting up of Commissions and consideration of their reports is no panacea. In 1990, the combined New York churches and their leaders produced evidence to the Mayor of what they described as massive police corruption involving blackmail netting some $5,000,000 each year. They chose to complain to the Mayor rather than the Police Commissioners who "... have always smothered such things [revelations] in the past".

Many theories have been put forward about the origins of institutionalised corruption and this author, beyond stating the obvious that it must come down in the end to human nature, does not wish and, indeed, is not qualified to put forward any fresh ones. However, a brief review of some current theories may be worth considering.

Training

In the past, probably before the possibility of a policeman becoming corrupt was even in contemplation, there was little, if any, formal instruction on the dangers awaiting the new recruit when once released upon the public. With regard to the relatively small proportion of officers who eventually became corrupt, it is doubtful that early training in the habit of integrity would have deterred most of them who were easily corruptible. Increasing emphasis on ethical behaviour during the early years of service is bound to have at least some good effect, but its absence in the past cannot be taken as a reason for a slide into criminality of earlier recruits. This lack of guidance has persisted and the Wood Commission drew attention to it in describing the evidence of a group of young officers who had become aware of misbehaviour among older colleagues. In essence, they said that there had been no effective ethical guidance in their basic training and that when they reported wrongful behaviour by more senior police, the reaction of their contemporaries was mostly unfavourable. Some were denied any personal contact, one was the subject of notices in the police station naming him as a plant, others were isolated and ignored. In such a negative atmosphere with no background of ethical training, the possibility of new officers being obliged to adopt the prevailing culture of group self-protection, the code of silence and step-by-step entry into dishonesty is very great. "Thou shalt not rock the boat", is a maxim drummed into the newly graduated officer, and woe betide those who choose to ignore it.

As against the suggestion that ethical standards can be effectively inculcated, is the results of a survey conducted among officers on their perception of corruption. Not only were they doubtful about the persuasive value of regulation, but equally so regarding rhetoric about integrity. The general view of those surveyed was that the maintenance of personal integrity was very much a private struggle. In those services which do provide some instruction into the overwhelming need for integrity, such as the Metropolitan Police seminars conducted by officers from CIB3, it appears that an effective means of driving the message home to established staff can be devised who are now beginning to show signs of an improved perception of the problem. The watch words of the initiative are that "Integrity is non-negotiable", a useful reminder in the nature of a mantra.

Detailed case studies of serious corruption situations would underline the ways in which vulnerable officers have been ensnared into criminal activities by dishonest colleagues, and found themselves convicted, disgraced and imprisoned. In the last analysis, when ethical standards in ordinary life are abandoned, there is only fear of discovery and punishment to deter people from committing crime. There is no reason to believe that police officers are any different in that respect from everyone else.

Internal Supervision

Lack of effective supervision has been put forward by authorities, usually from outside the police service, as the principal reason for corruption beginning and continuing in the service and there can be no doubt that it has played a substantial role in almost every instance of malpractice. But lack of proper supervision can only be blamed in limited circumstances, and certainly not in the major instances where very senior officers, whose primary function was supervision and leadership of their people, were themselves at the head of the dishonesty. Ex-Commander Drury could hardly be categorised as a weak leader, nor could it be suggested that he was incapable of exercising powerful supervision when the occasion demanded. Nor do circumstances suggest that he had adopted a *laissez faire* policy towards the activities of those under his command but, rather, that he was in firm control. Unwillingness to operate anti-corruption control among senior staff may sometimes be a factor as in the events taking place in the 75th Precinct, where everyone knew but no one acted.

External Supervision

There is a clear need, already recognised, that some form of independent oversight of police services is desirable. To be effective, the overseeing body needs to be free from interference from both inside and outside the service in order to maintain true independence. It must have sharp and persuasive teeth. Perhaps more important is the ability to carry police officers along with its aims and objectives, because the typical police "them and us" attitude towards it would be a serious obstruction to its efforts.

The Rotten Apple

Once again, there is a small element of truth lurking behind the theory in that a dishonest individual may well corrupt an honest one given time, circumstances and a receptive subject. The biological reaction of over-ripe fruit in the captive environment of a barrel is a wholly different matter to the corruption of a human being with free will and the capacity to walk away.

The "rotten apple" notion has been demolished by more than one authoritative writer as a feeble excuse for its advocate's own command failures. As long ago as 1972, in the Knapp Commission's report into corruption in the New York Police Department, it was considered that the "rotten apple" excuse had actually prevented reform.

> "According to this theory, which bordered on official Department doctrine, any policeman found to be corrupt must promptly be denounced as a rotten apple in an otherwise clean barrel. It must never be admitted that his individual corruption may be symptomatic of underlying disease ..."

It is mostly those who represent the interests of police in a role similar to a trades union, for example some UK Police Federation representatives who, understandably, cling to the rotten apple excuse, but they are not alone for politicians too have been known to support it when convenient.

Money

Representative organisations whose main regard is the welfare of their members can generally be relied upon to claim that better pay would bring improvements, even in the field of corruption. If there was any merit in this argument, it would have to be on the basis that their members were so badly paid as to be below the poverty line and obliged to supplement a niggardly wage by crime. In Third World countries with a huge gulf between those who have and those who have not, police officers are frequently at a very low level on the economic scale; it is also true that such countries will usually tolerate a culture of corruption among public officials who need to supplement their near starvation wages. If need was the driving force of corruption in developed nations, what of the corruption to be found among people earning considerable salaries in industry, political life and public services? As a factor in the reasons for corruption, salaries can only be put forward with tongue firmly in cheek.

Many of the illustrations of corrupt practices in this work have, as their *raison d'être*, the obtaining of some financial advantage, whilst others were for the purpose of some other benefit such as advancement or the possibility of some future patronage. Examples of what may constitute corruption are so many and diverse that to attempt an all-embracing definition of the word would be difficult and so full of ambiguities as to be little value. To adopt the *cliché* "... it is easier to recognise an elephant than describe it", is simpler and probably just as useful as an incomplete definition. The shortest and most simplistic is that any abuse of power which results in what most people would regard as unfairness, should be recognised as corrupt.

Fear

To introduce the concept of fear may well be controversial but, in the cold light of reason, the deterrent effect of detection and punishment prevents many waverers from indulging in crime, and once again, police officers are unlikely to be different from others in that respect.

To attempt to catalogue all the possible measures of

control suggested by those whose task it is do so would be equally fruitless, because a programme which was effective in the UK would not necessarily be of use in Australia. Nor would the measures taken in the NYPD be effective in, say, New Zealand. Their history and cultures are too different, as are the perceptions of the police by the populations they serve.

Judge Mollen, in the course of his inquiry into problems with the NYPD, said in regard to the long-term effects of reform:

> "The challenge we face is to maintain that commitment long after this Commissioner departs and the glare of public scrutiny subsides. We believe that the Department cannot contain that commitment alone. If history proves anything, it is that when the glare of scrutiny shines on the Department it can and will police successfully itself. But history also proves that left to its own devices the Department will backslide, and its commitment to integrity will erode."

In this penetrating analysis of the ephemeral nature of many reforms, read "Police Service" instead of "Department" and it will serve well as a word of caution to the police service of every civilised nation.

Appendix 1

The Indictment

John Meiklejohn, 38, Nathaniel Druscovitch, 37, and William Palmer, 43, for that they well knowing that Harry Benson and others had forged and uttered a certain warrant drawn by Vallot de Vitry le Francois for 20,000 francs and of which forgery the said Harry Benson and others have been convicted did feloniously receive, harbour, maintain and assist them. Those prisoners were also detained on the charge that they, well knowing that one Harry Benson and others had feloniously forged and uttered a certain warrant for £10,000, payable to Joseph Francis or order, and of which forgery the said Harry Benson and others had since been convicted, did feloniously receive, harbour, maintain and assist them.

They were all further detained for that they, well knowing that one Harry Benson and others had feloniously forged and uttered a certain warrant for £10,000, payable to Joseph Francis or order, did feloniously receive, harbour, maintain and assist them.

They were all further charged with conspiring together with Harry Benson and others, by divers subtle and corrupt means to prevent and avoid the lawful apprehension of the said Harry Benson and others, and thereby defeating the due course of law and justice.

Appendix 2

Public Interest Disclosure Act 1998

This legislation should be read with the Employment Rights Act 1996, part IV, which provides the legal remedies available to those who suffer detriment for revealing matters of public interest. The general object of the legislation is to protect the worker from unfair dismissal either openly or spuriously under the cloak of redundancy.

Protected Disclosure

Section 1 of the Act defines a "qualifying disclosure" as being any disclosure of information which, in the reasonable belief of the worker making the disclosure, tends to show one or more of the following:

Subsection (1)

- (a) that a criminal offence has been committed, is being committed or is likely to be committed,
- (b) that a person has failed, is failing or is likely to fail to comply with any legal obligation to which he is subject,
- (c) that a miscarriage of justice has occurred, is occurring or is likely to occur,
- (d) that the health and safety of any individual has been, is being or is likely to be endangered,
- (e) that the environment has been, is being or is likely to be damaged, or
- (f) that information tending to show any matter falling within any one of the preceding paragraphs has been, is being or is likely to be deliberately concealed.

Subsection (2)
For the purposes of subsection (1), it is immaterial whether the relevant failure occurred, occurs or would occur in the United Kingdom or elsewhere, or whether the law applying to it is that of the United Kingdom or of any other territory or country.

Subsection (3)
A disclosure is not a qualifying disclosure if the person making the disclosure commits an offence by making it.

Section 2
Subsection (1)
A worker has the right not to be subjected to any detriment by any act, or deliberate failure to act, by his employer done on the ground that the worker has made a protected disclosure.

Appendix 3

Regina v. Kellam, ex parte South Wales Police Authority

In the UK Queen's Bench Divisional Court the above-named case was heard by Mr Justice Richards, who gave judgment in favour of a police officer who had retired from the police force on medical grounds. In his judgment he said that the officer had retired from the police force because of stress caused by incidents of victimisation he received at work after his wife, also a police officer, had made allegations of malpractice in her unit.

The force medical officer had found that the officer was permanently disabled, but that was not as a result of an injury received in the execution of his duty, with the consequence that the officer was not entitled to a policeman's injury award under the 1987 regulations. The officer appealed against this decision and Dr A.M.P. Kellam, the police pensions' medical referee allowed the officer's appeal, finding that the stress causing his incapacity had been received within the meaning of reg.A11(1).

The police authority submitted that Dr Kellam had applied the wrong legal tests and asked for his decision to be overturned; however, the Judge, setting out the reasons for his decision, dismissed the application. The effect of the judgment is that there must be a causal connection between the person's service as an officer and the events rendering him unfit, but that the word "duty" in the regulation was not to be given a narrow meaning. It is sufficient for there to be a causal connection with service as an officer: it is not necessary to establish that work circumstances were the sole cause of injury.

Appendix 4

Police Integrity Commission Act 1966, s.5

Police Misconduct

(1) For the purposes of this Act, police misconduct means misconduct (by way of action or inaction or alleged action or inaction) of a police officer.

(a) whether or not it also involves non-police participants, and
(b) whether or not it occurs while the officer is officially on duty, and
(c) whether or not it occurred before the commencement of this section, and
(d) whether or not it occurred outside the State or outside Australia.

(2) Examples
Police misconduct can involve (but is not limited to) any of the following:

(a) police corruption,
(b) the commission of a criminal offence by a police officer,
    (b1) misconduct in respect of which the Commissioner of Police may take action under Part 9 of the Police Services Act 1990,
(c) corrupt conduct within the meaning of the Independent Commission Against Corruption 1988 Act involving a police officer,
(d) any other matters about which a complaint may be made under the Police Services Act 1990.

(3) Former Police Officers

Conduct may be dealt with, or continue to be dealt with, under the Act even though any police officer involved has ceased to be a police officer. Accordingly, references in this Act to a police officer extend, where appropriate, to include a former police officer.

Bibliography

Critical Years at the Yard	Belton Cobb	Fabers	1941
British Police and the Democratic Ideal	Charles Reith	OUP	1943
Detective Days	Frederick P. Wensley	Cassell	1931
Flying Squad	George "Jack" Frost	Rockliff	1948
The Fatal Shore	Robert Hughes	Pan Books	1987
Crime in London	Gilbert Kelland	Grafton Books	1986
In the Office of Constable	Sir Robert Mark	Collins	1978
Concise Oxford Dictionary of Quotations		OUP	1964
The Royal Commission Report into the New South Wales Police Service (The Wood Report)	The Rt. Honourable Justice J.R.T. Wood		1997
Longmans History of the United States of America	Hugh Brognan	Longman	1985

The City of New York Commission to Investigate Allegations of Police Corruption and Anti-corruption Procedures of the Police Department (The Mollen Report)	The Honourable Milton Mollen	1994

Index